Life of Fred®

Ice Cream

Life of Fred®
Ice Cream

Stanley F. Schmidt, Ph.D.

Polka Dot Publishing

ISBN: 978-1-937032-02-9

Library of Congress Catalog Number: 2011918583
Printed and bound in the United States of America

Polka Dot Publishing   Reno, Nevada

Order Life of Fred Books from:
JOY Center of Learning
http://www.LifeofFredMath.com

Questions or comments? Email the author at lifeoffred@yahoo.com

Sixth printing

Life of Fred: Ice Cream was illustrated by the author with additional clip art furnished under
license from Nova Development Corporation, which holds the copyright to that art.

for Goodness' sake

or as J.S. Bach—who was
never noted for his plain
English—often expressed it:

Ad Majorem Dei Gloriam
(to the greater glory of God)

If you happen to spot an error that the author, the publisher, and the printer missed, please let us know with an email to: lifeoffred@yahoo.com

As a reward, we'll email back to you a list of all the corrections that readers have reported.

A Note Before We Begin
Life of Fred: Ice Cream

Grades, diplomas, trophies, degrees, money, pats on the head, extra time watching television, memberships in honor societies, math ribbons, valedictorian, applause, student of the week, the "I can do all the honey cards in less than 57 seconds" button, the Fields Medal,* assistant professor, associate professor, full professor, finishing a three-unit course in British literature—these are all *performance goals*.

Mastering the multiplication tables, figuring out how to compute $\sum_{i=1}^{6} i$, understanding the differences between a formal letter and a personal letter, learning where Cyprus is on a map of the Mediterranean Sea or which two countries make up the Iberian Peninsula, or how to count back change**—these are all *learning goals*.

There is a world of difference between *performance goals* and *learning goals*.

The only way that they are alike is that they are both pleasurable.

---

* You can't get a Nobel prize in mathematics. Alfred Nobel, who lived in the 1800s, made his fortune in explosives. He was a practical sort of fellow. In his will, he established annual prizes in five areas: Physics, Chemistry, Medicine, Literature, and Peace. One story says that Nobel didn't think math was a practical subject—something you would ever use in everyday life.

It is an established fact that Alfred Nobel never read any of the Life of Fred series in which Fred experiences situations in his everyday life which require mathematics. Instead of Alfred Nobel prizes, there should be Fred Nobel prizes.

The Fields Medal isn't awarded annually, but quadrennially (a word you will encounter several times in this book). It is sometimes called "the Nobel Prize of Mathematics." On one side of the medal is a picture of Archimedes and his words: *Transire suum pectus mundoque potiri.* This is slightly weird since Archimedes didn't speak Latin. If your knowledge of Latin is like that of Archimedes, I will translate: *Rise above yourself and grasp the world.* Mathematics does a lot of world-grasping.

** These are all covered in this book.

Performance Goals

If you have just been hired at Harry's Hamburgers, all day long you will flip hamburgers, and you will ask customers, "Would you like fries with that?" You put in the hours, and they offer you the rewards of wages (10¢/hour), raises (11¢/hour), and titles (Junior Associate Team Leader).

Many math curricula operate the same way. All day long you do routine problems, and you get the gold stars, a diploma, and the grade.

Learning Goals

You learn for the joy of learning. That's why kids play with toys. They don't do it to earn stuff. No one needs to get external encouragement to go play on the swings and slides.

WHAT DO YOU WANT FOR YOUR CHILD?

Is the whole point to get through the book? This is the classic performance goal. Does your praise revolve around how many were answered correctly or how fast the pages were turned? Do you offer a "paycheck" in the form of treats? If so, when they grow up they will be good little workers at Harry's Hamburgers.

Or is the whole point that the book goes through them? Do you encourage discussion of the things that are being learned? Is learning where the joy is?

Kids with *performance goals* want easy successes. If they encounter non-routine problems, they want to cry or quit. Working hard means that they are dumb.

For kids with *learning goals,* exertion is positive. They don't blame anything when they hit a problem that takes 15 minutes to figure out. It's part of the road to mastery. You have seen it when kids are playing with little plastic blocks. They will spend hours fiddling with them.

Mathematics is not easy but neither is water skiing or backpacking. The whole point is to enjoy the difficulties and challenges—not to say that you have done it.

At the dinner table, talk about what Fred is doing, not about how many lessons were finished.

Contents

Chapter 1   Sunshine.. 13
                   sweet-smelling sleeping bag
                   counting by fours
                   remembering six times eight
                   stationary vs. *stationery*
                   the big question in arithmetic
                   two-digit multiplication
                   why a pound of hamburger weighs more than a
                       pound of gold

Chapter 2   Trimmed Down Table.......................... 19
                   learning up to 30×30
                   roosters and egg laying
                   easy way to learn 7×8
                   a clean desktop
                   sigma notation

Chapter 3   On His Desk.................................... 25
                   pronouncing French words that end in *t*
                   subtracting ounces from pounds
                    forestland in the United States
                   what five-year-olds think is funny vs. what
                       twenty-five-year olds think is funny
                   what isn't news
                    hyperbole isn't lying

Chapter 4   Mail. 31
                   bar graphs
                    letter openers for nine-month-olds
                    writing formal letters
                    capitalization in closing salutations
                    personal letters
                    elements of a set

Chapter 5 An Opportunity. 37
      special delivery emails
      why Stan couldn't fly to Kansas
      elapsed time
      ordered pairs, first and second coordinates
      numbers vs. numerals

Chapter 6 Ties & Shoes. 43
      a ways to do one thing and *b* ways to do a second
        imply *ab* ways to do both.
      why the times sign (×) is not used in algebra
      how to polish leather shoes
      subtracting minutes from hours

Chapter 7 A Map. 49
      artists looking at a map
      war historians looking at a map
      mathematicians looking at a map
      lovers of cheese looking at a map
      historians of literature looking at a map
      the promised land vs. Wisconsin
      easy way to remember 6 × 9
      agitating one's endoplasmic reticulum
      figuring out what "the land of milk and honey"
        might really have meant
      subtracting inches from feet

Chapter 8 Sand Castles in Cyprus. 55
      where Cyprus is located on a map
      Betty's attempt to get Fred to eat something
      87 flavors and 6 kinds of cones
      the cardinality of the set of all ice cream flavors
        beginning with the Greek letter alpha (α)

Chapter 9 The Right Machine. 61
      explicit vs. *implicit*
      Iberian Peninsula
      where to find an ibex
      two inches ≈ 5 centimeters
      selecting an ice cream maker—six questions
      seconds, minutes, and hours in the metric system

Chapter 10   Ingredients. 67
               how to find one-half of a large number
               how to get ice in the summer in Kansas in 1843
               drops, teaspoons, tablespoons, ounces, cups, quarts

Chapter 11   Seat Belts. 73
               where *not* to ride if you can't fit in the car
               graphing ordered pairs
               why you shouldn't park on the sidewalk
               subtracting ounces from gallons

Chapter 12   PieOne. 79
               perimeter of a building when not all the dimensions
                   are given
               why math was created
               area of a rectangle
               a poor way to teach ice cream eating

Chapter 13   Before Four. 85
               why Stanthony thought Chico Marx was Italian
               division by two-digit numbers
               speaking ironically
               Hooke's law
               slope of a line

Chapter 14   Starting the Machine. 91
               different scales on a graph
               given (40, 3) and (280, 21) and estimating (800, ?)
               domain and codomain
               how many digits should be in a serial number

Chapter 15   Booths at the Conference. 97
               uses for pizza buttons
               counting back change
               definition of liberty (it doesn't mean just freedom)
               ∪ is commutative

Chapter 16   Fast Freeze. 103
                  inequalities: < and >
                  how to eat pizza after eating a quart of ice cream
                  homogenized milk
                  why we use soap
                  cryogenics
                  the difference between liquid and superfluid
                  graph paper for those with lots of casual cash

Chapter 17   Joe and Ice Cream. 109
                  what protein and calcium are good for
                  subtracting ounces from quarts
                  expressing remainders as fractions
                  nothing physical is infinite

Chapter 18   Fred Orders a Pizza. 115
                  changing ounces to pounds and ounces
                  a pizza without calories
                  changing seconds into minutes and seconds

Chapter 19   Sugar. 121
                  to be jealous and to covet
                  five gallons of Sluice each day
                  making estimates using graphing

Index. 125

Chapter One
Sunshine

Fred's sleeping bag smelled good. Hanging it out on a tree in the Kansas air and sunshine was a good thing. Fred never knew that you were supposed to do something with a sleeping bag besides just sleep in it.

Fred owned an 85-year calendar. Since he was five years old, that calendar would last until he was 90. At that point, he imagined he would buy another calendar.

$$\begin{array}{r} 85 \\ + 5 \\ \hline 90 \end{array}$$

He had owned his sleeping bag for four years. Airing out his sleeping bag every four years seemed like a great idea. He was now five years old. He would air it out when he was 9. Then when he was 13. Then 17, 21, 25, 29, etc.

He wrote "air out sleeping bag" on every fourth year of his 85-year calendar. Then he wouldn't forget.

Fred flossed his teeth every evening, so that was easy to remember. He also easily remembered, "Six times eight is 48, and that is really great." (One use of poetry is to help people remember things. "In fourteen ninety-two, Columbus sailed the ocean blue.")

But when something happens only once every four years, the safest thing to do is write it down so you won't forget it.

Fred had read a lot of books. He knew a lot about math, history, poetry, science, art, geography, vexillology (the study of flags), Shakespeare, the Bible, economics, and beekeeping. But he had never read a book about sleeping bags.

Fred Didn't Know . . .

1. He might not fit into his three-foot sleeping bag when he turned 13.

2. If you sleep in the same sleeping bag every night for twenty or thirty years, it just might wear out.

3. Kids' sweat and adults' sweat are different.* Many adults air out their sleeping bags every morning rather than quadrennially (quad-DREN-knee-al-lee—once every four years).

---

* This is covered in more detail in *Life of Fred: Pre-Algebra 1 with Biology*

An 85-year calendar is hard to find in most stationery stores.* (An understatement.) One reason is that if you sell 85-year calendars, you will probably never have repeat customers.

Another reason is that 85-year calendars are pretty thick. They might be hard to hang on the wall.

How thick? How many months would be in an 85-year calendar.** There are 12 months in a year. Do we add, subtract, multiply, or divide? That's always **the big question in arithmetic**.

> **If you don't know whether to add, subtract, multiply or divide, first restate the problem with really simple numbers.**

Using really simple numbers—suppose there are 4 months in a year and we have a two-year calendar. Even without thinking, we know that would be 8 months. How did we get that? We multiplied.

So with an 85-year calendar and 12 months in a year, we need to multiply.

---

* *Stationery* (with an *e*) means writing paper and envelopes.
Stationary (with an *a*) means not moving.

How can you remember which is which? One way is to remember that **e**nvelopes are station**e**ry.

** You may have also noticed that *calendar* is spelled *calendAr*. English is strange. The way I remember that it is . . . I can't remember how I remember that. I just do.

$$\begin{array}{r} 85 \\ \times\ \ 12 \\ \hline \end{array}$$

We've never done this before. It is multiplying by a two-digit number.

$12 = 10 + 2$

It is multiplying by 2 and multiplying by 10.

Here's how it's done . . .

$$\begin{array}{r} {}^{1}85 \\ \times\ \ 12 \\ \hline 170 \end{array}$$

First, you multiply by 2. That we have seen before.

$$\begin{array}{r} 85 \\ \times\ \ 12 \\ \hline 170 \\ 85 \end{array}$$

Next, we multiply by the 1. (Since it's really 10, and not 1, we move the answer over one space to the left.)

And then just total things up.

$$\begin{array}{r} 85 \\ \times\ 12 \\ \hline 170 \\ 85 \\ \hline 1020 \end{array}$$

There are 1,020 months in an 85-year calendar.
There are 1,020 pages in an 85-year calendar.

One thousand, twenty pages!

Your Turn to Play

1. I buy my paper by the ream. One ream = 500 sheets. How many sheets would be in two reams of paper?

2. A ream of paper is about 5 cm thick. (I just measured it.) How thick would 2 reams be?

3. A ream of paper is about 2 inches thick. (I just measured it with the other side of my ruler.) How thick would 2 reams be?

More people in the world understand 5 cm than understand 2 inches.

Centimeters (cm) are part of the metric system. In the metric system (meters, liters, grams) everything is done by tens. For example, a centimeter is one-hundredth of a meter.

In the imperial system (feet, gallons, pounds) nothing is predictable.

36 inches = 3 feet = 1 yard

8 pints = 4 quarts = 1 gallon

16 ounces = 1 pound

12 troy ounces = 1 troy pound

> A pound of hamburger weighs more than a pound of gold.

(Gold is measured in troy ounces.)

........**ANSWERS**.......

1. There are two ways you could have done this problem.

By addition:
$$\begin{array}{r} 500 \\ +\ 500 \\ \hline 1000 \end{array}$$

By multiplication:
$$\begin{array}{r} 500 \\ \times\ \ \ 2 \\ \hline 1000 \end{array}$$

There are 1,000 sheets of paper in two reams.

2. By addition:
$$\begin{array}{r} 5 \\ +\ 5 \\ \hline 10 \end{array}$$

By multiplication:
$$\begin{array}{r} 5 \\ \times 2 \\ \hline 10 \end{array}$$

3. Two reams would be four inches.

A Row of Practice. *Do the whole row before you look at the answers.*

$$\begin{array}{r} 48 \\ +\ 75 \\ \hline 123 \end{array} \qquad \begin{array}{r} 748 \\ -\ 9 \\ \hline 739 \end{array} \qquad \begin{array}{r} 78 \\ \times 2 \\ \hline 156 \end{array} \qquad \begin{array}{r} 47 \\ \times 13 \\ \hline 141 \\ 47 \\ \hline 611 \end{array}$$

Chapter Two
Trimmed Down Table

Fred took out his honey cards and ran through the 36 multiplication facts. It took him less than a minute. Practicing over the years made it as easy as doing the ABCs.

There are happy ways to learn math and there are ways that are a torture. Before Fred started teaching at KITTENS University, the former math teacher would begin the first class by writing on the board:

×	1	2	3	4	5	6	7	8	9	10	11	12	13	14	15	16	17	18	19	20
1	1	2	3	4	5	6	7	8	9	10	11	12	13	14	15	16	17	18	19	20
2	2	4	6	8	10	12	14	16	18	20	22	24	26	28	30	32	34	36	38	40
3	3	6	9	12	15	18	21	24	27	30	33	36	39	42	45	48	51	54	57	60
4	4	8	12	16	20	24	28	32	36	40	44	48	52	56	60	64	68	72	76	80
5	5	10	15	20	25	30	35	40	45	50	55	60	65	70	75	80	85	90	95	100
6	6	12	18	24	30	36	42	48	54	60	66	72	78	84	90	96	102	108	114	120
7	7	14	21	28	35	42	49	56	63	70	77	84	91	98	105	112	119	126	133	140
8	8	16	24	32	40	48	56	64	72	80	88	96	104	112	120	128	136	144	152	160
9	9	18	27	36	45	54	63	72	81	90	99	108	117	126	135	144	153	162	171	180
10	10	20	30	40	50	60	70	80	90	100	110	120	130	140	150	160	170	180	190	200
11	11	22	33	44	55	66	77	88	99	110	121	132	143	154	165	176	187	198	209	220
12	12	24	36	48	60	72	84	96	108	120	132	144	156	168	180	192	204	216	228	240
13	13	26	39	52	65	78	91	104	117	130	143	156	169	182	195	208	221	234	247	260
14	14	28	42	56	70	84	98	112	126	140	154	168	182	196	210	224	238	252	266	280
15	15	30	45	60	75	90	105	120	135	150	165	180	195	210	225	240	255	270	285	300
16	16	32	48	64	80	96	112	128	144	160	176	192	208	224	240	256	272	288	304	320
17	17	34	51	68	85	102	119	136	153	170	187	204	221	238	255	272	289	306	323	340
18	18	36	54	72	90	108	126	144	162	180	198	216	234	252	270	288	306	324	342	360
19	19	38	57	76	95	114	133	152	171	190	209	228	247	266	285	304	323	342	361	380
20	20	40	60	80	100	120	140	160	180	200	220	240	260	280	300	320	340	360	380	400

Six students fainted. Three broke into tears.

It makes a big difference how it's taught.

Fred knew that it was really important to learn just the multiplication facts that pop up most often in everyday life. Memorizing what seventeen times nineteen equals is not one of them.

Here is Fred's trimmed down table:

×	1	2	3	4	5	6	7	8	9	10	11	12	13	14	15	16	17	18	19	20
1																				
2		4	6	8	10	12	14	16	18											
3			9	12	15	18	21	24	27											
4				16	20	24	28	32	36											
5					25	30	35	40	45											
6						36	42	48	54											
7							49	56	63											
8								64	72											
9									81											
10																				
11																				
12		24	36	48	60	72	84	96	108		132	144								
13																				
14																				
15																				
16																				
17																				
18																				
19																				
20																				

We need the 12-times table because a dozen comes up fairly frequently: inches/feet, months/years, and eggs. When a recipe calls for six dozen eggs, you automatically know that means 72 eggs.*

Okay hens. Get busy!

Roosters don't lay eggs.

Fred didn't have 12 × 10 in his trimmed down table. There is no need to memorize any

---

* Larger families never buy just one dozen eggs.

of the 10 times facts. They are so easy. 12×10 = 120. Just add a zero.

And the 11 times tables are also super easy. $2 \times 11 = 22$, $3 \times 11 = 33$, $4 \times 11 = 44$, etc.

Fred put away his honey cards. Just a minute a day keeps all the multiplication facts alive and sharp in his head.

Tomorrow, he was going to teach the last ten facts (6 times table up through 9 times table) to his arithmetic class. He would have the class make honey cards.

Three of the ten facts were pretty easy to remember.

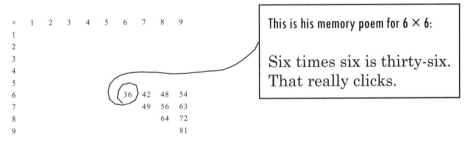

×	1	2	3	4	5	6	7	8	9
1									
2									
3									
4									
5									
6						36	42	48	54
7							49	56	63
8								64	72
9									81

This is his memory poem for **6 × 6**:

Six times six is thirty-six.
That really clicks.

We had already seen Fred's way to memorize 6 × 8:

> **Six times eight is 48,**
>
> **And that is really great.**

The other one that Fred liked was $7 \times 8 = 56$. He just remembered 7–8–5–6. The digits were almost in order. Seven and eight gives you five and six. Some of his students liked that, and others thought it was too silly.

Fred's desktop was cleaner than most of the other faculty members' desktops. One teacher down the hall had three empty coffee cups, a half-eaten sandwich, cookies, candies, and crackers on his desk.

Fred didn't own any coffee cups, and all his food was stuffed into his desk drawers.

Some teachers had their desks covered with their lecture notes, homework papers that needed to be corrected, and bills that needed to be paid.

Fred kept his lecture notes in binders that were on one of his bookshelves. The students' homework papers were in a small cardboard box on the floor. Fred liked to sit on the floor and read the homework. Lying on his tummy on the floor was one of his favorite positions. Being five years old makes a difference. Not too many other teachers did that.

flexible

Fred could put his leg behind his head. Sometimes he did this while he was sitting at his desk. It took some students a while to get used to having a teacher who was five years old. And for some it took a while to get used to having a teacher with his leg behind his head as he explained sigma notation.[*]

Your Turn to Play

1. What does $\sum\limits_{i=1}^{6} i$ equal? Work out your answer completely.

Σ is a capital S in Greek. It is called sigma. When you add two numbers, it is called finding the **sum**. Sigma reminds mathematicians of s̲um.

2. In real life, the sum of 5 apples and 6 apples is 11 apples. In algebra, 5y + 6y = 11y.

What does $\sum\limits_{i=1}^{6} iy$ equal? Work out your answer completely.

3. $5\overline{)3675}$

---

[*] Sigma notation is taught in Advanced Algebra.

$\sum\limits_{i=3}^{8} 7x^i$ is a short way of writing $7x^3 + 7x^4 + 7x^5 + 7x^6 + 7x^7 + 7x^8$.

$\sum\limits_{i=1}^{5} iy$ is a short way of writing $1y + 2y + 3y + 4y + 5y$.

1y (one y) is often shortened to just y.

```
.......ANSWERS.......
```

1. $\sum_{i=1}^{6} i = 1 + 2 + 3 + 4 + 5 + 6$

```
                                    1
                                    2
                                    3
                                    4
                                    5
                                  + 6
                                   21
```

2. $\sum_{i=1}^{6} iy = 1y + 2y + 3y + 4y + 5y + 6y = 21y$

```
        735
3. 5) 3675
      35
      17
      15
      25
      25
       0
```

A Row of Practice. *Do the whole row before you look at the answers.*

92	204	56	535
+ 78	− 9	× 23	+ 778
170	195	168	1313
		112	
		1288	

Chapter Three
On His Desk

Some teachers adorn their desks with photographs, trophies, and bibelots.* It's not hard to figure out why Fred didn't have a picture of a wife or of his kids on his desktop.

Fred kept his 85-year calendar on a chair next to his desk.

What was on his desk was . . . the Sunday newspaper—all 15 pounds of it. It looked like a log. All together, the news section, the sports section, the comics, and the business section weighed 12 ounces. The rest of the newspaper was advertisements.

How much did the ads weigh? What is 15 pounds minus 12 ounces?

$$
\begin{array}{r}
15 \text{ lbs.} \\
- \underline{\hspace{1cm} 12 \text{ oz.}}
\end{array}
$$

ballet

---

* A bibelot (BEE-ba-low) is some cute little object. Since the word *bibelot* comes from the French, the *t* at the end is not pronounced.

　　You don't pronounce the final *t* in *ballet* for the same reason.

When we subtracted 6 from 34

$$
\begin{array}{r}
34 \\
-\ 6 \\
\hline
\end{array}
\qquad \text{we borrowed ``one''} \qquad
\begin{array}{r}
^{2}\cancel{3}4 \\
-\ 6 \\
\hline
2\,8
\end{array}
$$

Similarly, when we subtract 12 oz. from 15 lbs. we will borrow one. One pound is the same as 16 ounces.

$$
\begin{array}{r}
15\ \text{lbs.} \\
-\ \quad 12\ \text{oz.} \\
\hline
\end{array}
\implies
\begin{array}{rr}
^{14}\cancel{15}\ \text{lbs.} & 16\ \text{oz.} \\
-\qquad & 12\ \text{oz.} \\
\hline
14\ \text{lbs.} & 4\ \text{oz.}
\end{array}
$$

Fourteen pounds, four ounces of the Sunday paper were ads.*

Fred turned to his favorite comic strip.

Teacher Tales

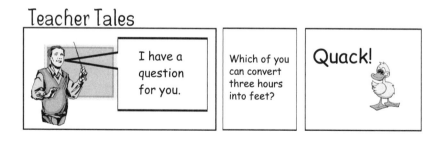

---

* We are not running out of forests in the United States. According to United States Forest Acreage Trendline (on the Internet), "The forest resources of the U.S. have continued improving in general condition and quality, as measured by increased average size and volume of trees. This trend has been evident since the 1960s and before. The total forestland acreage has remained stable since 1900."

We're not running out of trees.

Fred thought that was soooo funny. What five-year-olds think is funny is often not funny to twenty-five-year-olds.

Fred turned to the news section headlines:

Trouble in the Middle East

The Government Schools
and the Post Office Need
More Money

He looked at the science section headlines:

Computers Getting Faster

In the business section:

The Stock Market Remains Jittery

In the sports section:

Final Score: Merrywibbles beat the Twips 7–3

In other words, there was no new news.

Next Fred looked through the advertisements. Six pounds, nine ounces of the ads were for women's clothes.

$$
\begin{array}{ll}
14 \text{ lbs.} & 4 \text{ oz.} \\
- \ 6 \text{ lbs.} & 9 \text{ oz.} \\
\end{array}
\quad \Longrightarrow \quad
\begin{array}{ll}
 & 4+16 \\
13 & 20 \\
\cancel{14} \text{ lbs.} & \cancel{4} \text{ oz.} \\
- \ 6 & 9 \text{ oz.} \\
\hline
7 \text{ lbs.} & 11 \text{ oz.} \\
\end{array}
$$

That left 7 pounds, 11 ounces of ads that were not for women's clothes.

Fred skipped the grocery store ads. It had been a million years* since he had gone to the store to buy food.

He skipped the used car ads,
the wrinkle cream ads,
the real estate ads,
the jewelry ads,
the help-wanted ads, and
the furniture store ads.

Then he found an ad that excited him.

A ream of paper is 500 sheets.

---

* *A million years* is an example of hyperbole (high-PER-bow-lee). Hyperbole is an obvious exaggeration. It is clearly not meant to be taken literally. It is not a lie because the other person knows that you really don't mean 1,000,000 years.

Lying only happens when you mean to deceive the other person.

These Your-Turn-to-Play questions may require a little thought.

☞ In baby math books, you write the answers to the million questions as fast as you can scribble.

☞ In high school math books, some questions may take you five minutes to figure out.

☞ In college calculus, you are pretty fast if you can find the antiderivative of $\dfrac{1}{x^3 + 1}$ in under 30 minutes.

Your Turn to Play

1. How many sheets of paper in a case of paper?

2. If Fred uses 25 sheets of paper each day, how long would it take him to use up a case of paper?

3. If a ream of paper weighs 4 pounds, how much would a case of paper weigh?

4. $\displaystyle\sum_{i=4}^{7} i = ?$

You will not learn as much if you simply looked at the questions and then turned the page to read these answers.

. . . . ANSWERS . . . .

1. The advertisement said that there are 10 reams in a case. Each ream has 500 sheets. $10 \times 500 = 5,000$.

2. The question asks how long it would take to use up 5,000 sheets of paper if you were using 25 sheets per day.

If you don't know whether to add, subtract, multiply, or divide, first restate the problem using really simple numbers.

Suppose a case has 6 sheets of paper, and I was using 2 sheets/day. Then it would take me 3 days. I divided.

So with the original problem we divide 5,000 by 25.

$$
\begin{array}{r}
200 \\
25 \overline{)\,5000} \\
\underline{50} \\
00 \\
\underline{00} \\
00 \\
\underline{00}
\end{array}
$$

It would take Fred 200 days to use up a case of paper.

3. There are 10 reams in a case. Each ream weighs 4 pounds. $10 \times 4 = 40$. A case would weigh 40 pounds.

4. $\sum\limits_{i=4}^{7} i = 4 + 5 + 6 + 7 = 22$

Chapter Four
Mail

Fred reached into his desk drawer to get his scissors. He wanted to cut out that Office Junction ad for a case of paper.

Yesterday's mail was on top of the scissors. On Saturday he had been so busy investigating the idea of becoming a farmer and going to the pet store to get a goldfish that he hadn't had a chance to open his mail.

Forty letters were from people who had math questions for him. Fred's fame as a good math teacher had spread around the world. In the years that he had been teaching at KITTENS, he had been interviewed by many television and radio programs. His revolutionary teaching methods were described in numerous magazine articles.

There were also 60 fan letters, 10 invitations to speak at conferences, and 80 pieces of junk mail.

In a bar graph:

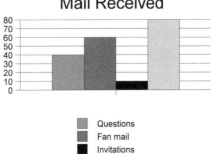

He took the 190 pieces of mail and put them on top of his desk. He got the scissors and cut out the Office Junction ad.

When he first became a teacher at KITTENS, the university offered him their beginning teacher's package: four file folders, a pen, a clipboard, a letter opener, and a box of paperclips.

The standard beginning teacher's package

However, since Fred was only nine months old when he started teaching at KITTENS,* they omitted the letter opener.

Being treated like a baby didn't bother Fred. He had something just as sharp as a steel letter opener that he could use.

He picked an envelope out of the pile. Sometimes he didn't know whether it was going to be a math

---

* The story is in *Life of Fred: Calculus.*

question, fan mail, an invitation or just junk mail. He nosed open the envelope. The letter was very formal.

McKloshy Fudge Company
123 Sweetie Lane
Wichita Kansas

February 9, 2011

Fred Gauss
Math Building
Room 314
KITTENS University
Kansas

Dear Sir:

I was reading in the fifth chapter of *LOF: Beginning Algebra Expanded Edition* about ordered pairs, such as (2,3).

I know that in sets, {2,3} is equal to {3,2}.

Is this also true for ordered pairs?

Very truly yours,

Mishneekoff McKloshy

Mishneekoff McKloshy

Formal letters (also known as business letters) have:

☆ full return address,

☆ full name and address of the person the letter is sent to,

☆ A colon (:) after the *Dear Sir,*

☆ The closing salutation is either *Yours truly,* or *Sincerely yours,* or *Very truly yours**, and

☆ The sender's name is both typed and signed.

Fred didn't have a typewriter, so he began to compose his answer on his computer.

Professor Fred Gauss
Math Building
Room 314
KITTENS University
Kansas

February 13, 2011

Mishneekoff McKloshy
McKloshy Fudge Company
123 Sweetie Lane
Wichita, Kansas

Dear Mr. McKloshy:

Then Fred changed his mind. This wasn't a situation that required a formal business letter.

Fred turned off his computer and took out a sheet of university stationery. He wrote a personal letter, not a business letter:

---

* Only the first word in the closing salutation is capitalized. Lots of people get that wrong.

KITTENS University
Kansas

2/13/2011

Dear Mishneekoff,

    An ordered pair, such as (2, 3), is ordered. The order matters. The ordered pair (3, 2) is different than (2, 3).

With my best wishes,
Fred

Your Turn to Play

1. Fred wrote 2/13/2011. This meant February 13, 2011. February is the second month of the year. Using Fred's style, how would you write March 22, 1965?

2. Is it true that {Б, Д, ☺ } = {Д, ☺, Б}?

3. Fred's opening salutation was *Dear Mishneekoff,* and he could have also used *Dear Mr. McKloshy,* and it still would have been a personal letter rather than a business letter. What is the indication that it is not a formal business letter?

4. If you receive a letter dated 5/1/2011, in what month was it written?

5. Your pet used to weigh 45 pounds. In order to lose weight, he took up skating and lost 7 ounces. How much does he now weigh?

........ANSWERS.......

1. March is the third month of the year.

January = 1

February = 2

March = 3

    March 22, 1965 can be written as 3/22/1965.

2. It is true that {Б, Д, ☺ } = {Д, ☺, Б}. The order in which you list the elements of a set does not matter. The only rule is that you should not list an element more than once. For example, don't write {Д, ☺, Б, ☺}.

    (*Elements* of a set means the same thing as *members* of a set.)

3. In business letters, the opening salutation uses a colon instead of a comma.

4. May is the fifth month.

5.

$$
\begin{array}{rr}
 & 45 \text{ lbs.} \\
- & 7 \text{ oz.} \\
\hline
\end{array}
\Rightarrow
\begin{array}{rrr}
 & \overset{44}{\cancel{45}} \text{ lbs.} & 16 \text{ oz.} \\
- & & 7 \text{ oz.} \\
\hline
 & 44 \text{ lbs.} & 9 \text{ oz.}
\end{array}
$$

A Row of Practice. *Do the whole row before you look at the answers.*

77	112	97	849
+ 59	− 8	× 53	+ 698
136	104	291	1547
		485	
		5141	

Chapter Five
An Opportunity

red's computer trembled. The monitor woke up and the speakers announced: `You have a special delivery email.` Fred thought to himself, *This must be urgent. I've never received a special delivery email before.*

He got out his clipboard and a pen in case he needed to take notes. Then he realized that this was on his computer. He turned on his printer so he could print out the message if he needed to.

EMERGENCY EMAIL-O-GRAM

From: Polka Dot Publishing <lifeoffred@yahoo.com>

To: Professor Fred Gauss

Subject: Conference Speaker Needed

Dearest Fred,

We've got a problem, and we need your help.

Quadrennially, Polka Dot Publishing hosts the Math and Pizza Conference. It's held on the second Sunday afternoon in February. (That's today!)

The conference is being held at PieOne Pizza near the KITTENS University campus.

We've just learned that our keynote speaker, Dr. Stan Schmidt, can't make it. He was supposed to fly into Kansas today from his home in Reno, Nevada. He couldn't get through the airport security. The guards told him to put up his arms so that they could pat him down. Every time they started patting his ribs, he nearly giggled to death. He was just too ticklish.

Could you fill in for him as speaker this afternoon? Forty-five minutes on any math or pizza topic. We would be so grateful.

◆◆◆Attachment◆◆◆
Remember to check for viruses

Stan hiding so they can't
tickle him anymore.

Wow! What an opportunity Fred thought to himself. *I'm just sad that I didn't get to see Stan. Maybe sometime when I'm in Reno, I'll meet him. I bet we would have a lot to talk about.*

Fred emailed Polka Dot Publishing and told them that he would be delighted to be the keynote speaker.

He knew that the Math and Pizza Conference would begin at four this afternoon. He had seen that on the posters that had been up all over the KITTENS campus.*

12:55 p.m.

It was now five minutes to one.

From 12:55 to 1:00 is 5 minutes.
From 1:00 to 4:00 is 3 hours.

Fred had three hours and five minutes to get ready.

Fred's first thought was *Which bow tie will I wear?* (Many people, when told they have a 45-minute speech to give three hours from now, would be concentrating on preparing the speech.)

Since Polka Dot Publishing was hosting this conference, Fred narrowed down his search

* Those posters had been put up three years, eleven months, and twenty-seven days ago—shortly after the previous quadrennial conference.

to his six polka dot bow ties. He thought that would be respectful.

Then came the question of whether he should wear his black shoes or his brown shoes.

Fred remembered Mishneekoff's letter about **ordered pairs**. The bow ties and shoes could be thought of as possible ordered pairs. The first choice was which bow tie, and the second choice was which shoe color.

Suppose the six polka dot bow ties were red, green, orange, blue, purple, and pink. Then one ordered pair might be (red, black). Another might be (red, brown) or (green, brown).

The first part of the ordered pair (called the **first coordinate**) represented the color of the bow tie. The **second coordinate** represented the color of the shoes.

(orange, black)

first coordinate   second coordinate

Fred had written to Mishneekoff, "*The order matters. The ordered pair (3, 2) is different than (2, 3).*"

The ordered pair (orange, black) is not the same as the ordered pair (black, orange).

Can you imagine Fred with a black bow tie and orange shoes?

Your Turn to Play

1. Fred had started thinking about the bow tie and the shoes that he would wear at 12:55. He made his final decision at 1:20. How long had it taken him to decide?

2. Fred had hundreds of bow ties in his collection. He kept them in a big box. He put the box on a scale. It weighed 37 lbs. Then he took the pink bow tie out of the box. How much did the scale now read? (The pink bow tie weighed 2 oz.)

3. The bow tie with pink polka dots was one of Fred's favorites. He had purchased it at a garage sale last year on September 13th. Today is February 13th. How many months ago did he buy that bow tie?

4. The email from Polka Dot Publishing asked Fred to speak for 45 minutes. If Fred spoke at the rate of 100 words per minute, how many words would he speak in 45 minutes?

from previous books . . .

5. $\{4, M\} \cup \{4, L\} = ?$

6. $3^2 = ?$

7. Write one million as a numeral.

8. $2xy + 7xy = ?$

. . . . ANSWERS . . . .

1. From 12:55 to 1:00 is 5 minutes.

   From 1:00 to 1:20 is 20 minutes.

It had taken Fred 25 minutes to decide.

2.

	37 lbs.		$\overset{36}{\cancel{37}}$ lbs.	16 oz.
$-$	2 oz.		$-$	2 oz.
			36 lbs.	14 oz.

The box now weighs 36 lbs., 14 oz.

3.   September

    October

    November   It was 5 months ago.

    December

    January

    February

4. If you don't know whether to add, subtract, multiply, or divide, restate the problem with simpler numbers.   Suppose he spoke for 2 minutes at the rate of 3 words per minute.   He would have spoken 6 words. We multiplied.

   In the original problem (45 minutes at the rate of 100 words per minute) we multiply 45×100.

   Fred would speak 4,500 words.

5. $\{4, M\} \cup \{4, L\} = \{4, M, L\}$ The union of two sets.

6. $3^2 = 3 \times 3 = 9$ 3 raised to the second power

7. One million as a numeral is 1,000,000.

8. $2xy + 7xy = 9xy$

Chapter Six
Ties & Shoes

Do you have a minute?

Before you begin this chapter, you have a little work to do to <u>earn the right</u> to continue reading Fred's adventures.

Here is the Official Procedure for honey/flash cards that you made in the previous book. You will now be using all the multiplication cards—all the way up to 9 × 9. If your dog ate the cards or the wind carried them away, turn back to Chapter 12 in the *Life of Fred: Honey* book and make a new deck of cards. That will take about three minutes.

Take each card and say (or guess) the answer and see if you got it right. Put the ones you got right in one pile and the ones you missed in another pile.

Now pick up the missed pile and repeat until all the cards end up in the I-got-it-right pile.

F red tried on his red polka dot bow tie and his black shoes. Then he tried on his green polka dot bow tie and his brown shoes. In 25 minutes he had tried on every combination.

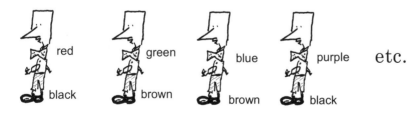

red   black

green   brown

blue   brown

purple   black

etc.

How many different combinations were there? How many different ordered pairs: (bow tie color, shoe color)?

There were 6 bow tie colors and 2 shoe colors.

Fred got organized and wrote them out:

(red, black)	(green, black)	(orange, black)	(blue, black)	(purple, black)	(pink, black)
(red, brown)	(green, brown)	(orange, brown)	(blue, brown)	(purple, brown)	(pink, brown)

His chart had two rows and six columns. There were 12 possible combinations—twelve ordered pairs.

In algebra—where we sometimes use letters to replace numbers—the rule is:

If there are *a* ways of doing one thing and *b* ways of doing another thing, then there are *ab* ways of doing both.

In algebra, *ab* means *a* times *b*.*

---

* In arithmetic we write 7 × 8 = 56. When we get to algebra, we have to stop using the times sign (×).

    You ask, "Why?"

    I answer, "In algebra we use both numbers and letters. One of our favorite letters is x. The problem is that × looks a lot like x. Suppose we want to write x times y. If we wrote x×y, some people might think we meant xxy.

    "So in algebra, if we want to write x times y, we will write xy."

Fred finally selected the pink polka dot bow tie and the brown shoes.

Now I'm ready to do my speech, Fred thought. Had he forgotten anything? He made a list:

pink

brown

✓ Shirt, shoes, pants, underwear, and bow tie.

✓ He knew where PieOne Pizza was. (He had been there many times in the last five years.)

✓ He knew how long he would be speaking: 45 minutes.

✓ It was now 1:20, so he had plenty of time until 4:00.

| From 1:20 to 2:00 is 40 minutes. |
| From 2:00 to 4:00 is 2 hours. |
| So Fred had two hours and forty minutes. |

✓ Teeth were already brushed this morning.

✓ Shoes were polished.*

There was a knock on the door. Betty and Alexander came into Fred's office.

They all had stories to tell. Betty and Alexander let Fred go first since he was the youngest.

---

* To polish leather shoes is a two-step process. Step #1: Buy a can of shoe polish that is the correct color. For black shoes, buy black polish. For brown shoes, buy brown polish. Step #2: Follow the directions on the can.

I love the word *polish*. Uncapitalized, *polish* (PAUL-ish) means to make something shine. Capitalized, *Polish* (POLE-ish) means the language spoken in the country of Poland. It is one of the few words in English that changes its pronunciation if you capitalize it.

Fred pointed to his sleeping bag
and remarked how clean it was.
Alexander said that it did smell better.

fresh & clean

Fred then showed them his honey cards
that he had invented. He said that it was the
easiest way to learn the multiplication tables.

Betty took the cards and said, "Time me."
She went through the 40 cards in 42 seconds.

Alexander asked, "Why do you call them
honey cards? I thought they were called flash
cards."

Fred explained that today in Sunday
school, they were studying
honey, and they learned
how to cut up a piece of
paper into eight little
rectangles.

Alexander asked again, "But what has that
got to do with honey?"

Fred explained, "Carrie, our Sunday school
teacher, had us draw pictures of bees on the
little rectangles. And bees make honey. And
then we had honey during snack time. She put
the honey on graham crackers. I didn't eat mine
because I wasn't very hungry.

"Oh, and we also learned that bees can
make their hives in the ground or in the bodies
of dead animals."

Betty had to remind herself that this was Sunday school for five-year-olds. Maybe they would get a little deeper into theology next year. (*Theology* = study of God)

Your Turn to Play

1. Betty could do Fred's forty honey cards in 42 seconds. Was she going faster or slower than one card per second?

2. $2^3 = ?$

3. When Betty and Alexander knocked on Fred's door, he had 2 hours and 40 minutes left before his speech. If the three of them talked for a total of 19 minutes, how much time would Fred have left before his speech?

4. If we started with 2 hours and 40 minutes and subtracted 50 minutes, how much time would be left?

5. $\sum_{i=3}^{8} ix = ?$

6. If Polka *Duck* Publishing had invited Fred to speak, Fred would pick one of his 47 duck bow ties. He would have chosen one of the 6 pairs of rubber shoes that he owned. Rubber shoes can go in water like ducks do. Usually, you don't want to get your leather shoes really wet.

How many possible outfits could Fred choose among?

. . . . ANSWERS . . . .

1. If Betty were doing one card per second, she would do all 40 cards in 40 seconds. Since it took her longer than 40 seconds to do the cards, she was going slower than one card per second.

2. $2^3 = 2 \times 2 \times 2 = 8$

3.

$$
\begin{array}{ll}
2 \text{ hrs.} & 40 \text{ min.} \\
- \qquad\quad & 19 \text{ min.} \\
\hline
2 \text{ hrs.} & 21 \text{ min.}
\end{array}
$$

4.

$$
\begin{array}{ll}
2 \text{ hrs.} & 40 \text{ min.} \\
- \qquad\quad & 50 \text{ min.}
\end{array}
\quad \Longrightarrow \quad
\begin{array}{ll}
\overset{1}{\cancel{2}} \text{ hrs.} & \overset{60+40}{\overset{100}{\cancel{40}}} \text{ min.} \\
- \qquad\quad & 50 \text{ min.} \\
\hline
1 \text{ hr.} & 50 \text{ min.}
\end{array}
$$

5. $\displaystyle\sum_{i=3}^{8} ix = 3x + 4x + 5x + 6x + 7x + 8x = 33x$

6. There are 47 ways to choose a duck bow tie. There are 6 ways to pick a pair of rubber shoes. There are 47×6 ways to do both.

$$
\begin{array}{r}
\overset{4}{4}7 \\
\times \quad 6 \\
\hline
282
\end{array}
\text{ ways to do both}
$$

Chapter Seven
A Map

Before you begin this chapter, you have a little work to do to <u>earn the right</u> to continue reading Fred's adventures. Do the honey cards until all the cards end up in the I-got-it-right pile.

Betty said, "It must have been Honey Sunday for the whole church. The sermon this morning was about the promised land. It was called the land of milk and honey."

Fred had a map on his wall of the Mediterranean Sea and the surrounding countries. (The map is on the next page.)

Fred had studied that map for many hours. He had also read a lot of history. If you were to point to any part of that map, Fred could tell you stories.

It Depends on Who Is Looking at the Map

An artist will see

✳ the early art of Egypt.

✳ the rebirth (Renaissance) in the 1300s to the 1600s in Europe (Italy, France, etc.).

A war historian will see

✳ the map completely filled with blood.

A mathematician will see

✳ In Greece, Euclid's geometry book (*Elements*, 300 BC) which had gone through more editions than any other book in world history except the Bible.

✳ All the famous mathematicians of Greece, Italy, France, Germany and the United Kingdom (U.K.), and Russia.

The Mediterranean Sea and the Surrounding Countries

A lover of cheese will see France.

A literature historian will see

✳ Spain as the birthplace of the first novel ever written (*Don Quixote*).

✳ The plays of ancient Greece.

✳ England's William Shakespeare.

On the right side of Fred's map was the promised land, "the land of milk and honey."

This seemed very strange to him. He asked Betty, "From what I've read, that land to the northeast of Egypt is hot and dry. There are no natural green fields where lots of cows can graze and bees can buzz. Wouldn't Wisconsin, which is loaded with green fields and cows, be a better spot to call the land of milk and honey?"

That was a tough question. Betty didn't have an answer.

small essay

Alexander's Answer

There are many ways to tell the truth. For five-year-olds, everything has to be quite literal. You remember the poem:

Six times nine is fifty-four.

Who could ask for anything more?

Solid, concrete, and true—that's great for 6×9 = 54.

But the big truths of life demand more than solid, concrete, and literally true.

I remember the first time I ever saw Betty. I didn't describe that event in my diary: Upon first seeing Betty, my heart rate increased, my blood pressure went up, I began to perspire, and the endoplasmic reticulum of my cells was agitated.

That would have been true . . . but really dumb.

Instead, I wrote a single sentence: *When I saw Betty for the first time, my heart stopped beating for a minute.*

My heart didn't literally stop beating, but these words of poetry more truly describe the event than any clinical description of my body.

So, in the same way, when those descendants of a man called Israel ("the children of Israel") had traveled through that desert land for forty years, what better way to describe the end of their journey than to call it a "land of milk and honey"?

Fred didn't quite understand Alexander's answer. Fred had never walked for forty years in the desert—hot and dry—through a land with no refrigerators. What turns into sweetened milk when there's no refrigeration?

ICE CREAM!!!

Now Fred had it all figured out.

Your Turn to Play

1. [Question for poets] The ten multiplication facts that we've introduced in this book are:

×	1	2	3	4	5	6	7	8	9
1									
2									
3									
4									
5									
6						36	42	48	54
7							49	56	63
8								64	72
9									81

We have also done a little poetry to make these facts easier to remember.

> Six times six is thirty-six.
> That really clicks.

> Six times eight is 48,
> And that is really great.

> Six times nine is 54.
> Who could ask for anything more?

Invent at least one more poem for any of the other seven multiplication facts.

2. $\sum\limits_{i=4}^{6} 3i = ?$

3. If your stack of homework was 5' 3" (that's five feet, three inches) tall and you did 7" of it. How tall would the remaining homework pile be?

.... ANSWERS ....

1. Here are some of my attempts. Yours will probably be better.

If you catch the flu
And say ahchoo,
Then 6 times 7 is 42.

You're really in a stew
If you don't know
that 6 times 7 is 42.

Six times seven is 42.
The wind blew and blew
                and blew.

2. $\sum\limits_{i=4}^{6} 3i = 3\times4 + 3\times5 + 3\times6 =$ $\begin{array}{r} 12 \\ 15 \\ +\ 18 \\ \hline 45 \end{array}$

3.

$$\begin{array}{ll} 5\text{ feet} & 3\text{ inches} \\ - & 7\text{ inches} \\ \hline \end{array}$$

$$\begin{array}{ll} \overset{4}{\cancel{5}}\text{ feet} & \overset{3+12}{\underset{15}{\cancel{3}}}\text{ inches} \\ - & 7\text{ inches} \\ \hline 4\text{ feet} & 8\text{ inches} \end{array}$$

A Row of Practice. *Do the whole row before you look at the answers.*

28	517	76	97	846
+ 78	− 78	× 58	× 7	+ 592
106	439	608	679	1438
		380		
		4408		

Chapter Eight
Sand Castles in Cyprus

<u>Earn the right</u> to continue reading Fred's adventures. Do the honey cards. It only takes about a minute.

The thought of ice cream reverberated in Fred's mind. It bounced around in his skull like a ping pong ball. His eyes turned into ice cream cones. He had seen the promised land, and it was . . . ice cream.

Betty attempted to interrupt Fred's reverie.*

She asked Fred, "Polka Dot Publishing is having their quadrennial conference at four o'clock this afternoon. Are you coming? We hear that Dr. Schmidt will be speaking."

Fred said, "No." Half of Fred's three-pound brain was still thinking about ice cream. All he had heard from Betty was, "Dr. Schmidt will be speaking."

Betty thought Fred was answering the question, "Are you coming?" So she asked Fred, "Why not?"

Fred answered, "Because he's too ticklish."

---

* REV-eh-ree Reverie is daydreaming, meditating, or having wonder-filled visions.

Fred started muttering, "Chocolate, vanilla, strawberry, caramel cashew, avocado, cherry vanilla, mocha fudge, fresh banana, peanut butter fudge, black raspberry, chocolate chip, cookie dough, pecan praline, black raspberry marble, chocolate marble, lemon chiffon, peppermint, black walnut, chocolate mint, rocky road, brownie nut fudge, bubble gum, coconut pineapple, mango, toasted almond, burgundy cherry, maple walnut, butter brickle, apple raisin strudel, apricot, blueberry, butterscotch, coconut, amaretto, mint chip, key lime, pumpkin, macadamia. . . ."

Fred had gone bonkers; he had gone off the deep end; he wasn't with it. Alexander's favorite expression when Fred was like this was, "Fred is building sand castles in Cyprus."

In case you've forgotten . . .

After several minutes, Fred left his reverie and joined the conversation with Betty and Alexander.

Betty repeated her question and Fred answered, "I've been looking forward to this conference for four years. Haven't you heard? Dr. Schmidt can't make it to the conference. They have asked me to give the keynote speech in his place."

Betty said, "That's too bad that Stan can't make it. What's going to be the topic of your speech?"

"It was just minutes ago that I learned that I'm supposed to be the main speaker," said Fred. "Polka Dot Publishing said that I could choose any math or pizza topic. I think I'll talk about ice cream."

Alexander couldn't believe what he was hearing. He sputtered, "But, but, but. . . ."

Betty told him he was starting to sound like a motorboat.

Alexander continued, "I've got two big questions for you, young man. First of all, you have never been interested in food. In all the years I've known you, you have never given a thought to food. Every time you have had food in front of you, you have stuck it in your pocket and said, 'For later.' You have never been hungry."

Alexander hadn't really asked a question. Implicit* in his statements was the question, "Why have you changed?"

Fred said, "Can you imagine wandering around in the hot, dry desert for 40 years and then getting a black raspberry marble ice cream cone?"

---

* Implicit = hidden inside of

Betty saw this as a golden opportunity. Fred might actually be willing to eat something! She had always been concerned about Fred's not growing. She suggested, "Why don't the three of us go out for some ice cream?"

"Could we head to King KITTENS?" Fred asked. "Polka Dot Publishing sent me $400 as an honorarium (honor-RARE-ee-um) for my speech. I know exactly what I want to get."

And off they headed to the largest shopping center in Kansas.

Betty imagined that they would be heading to KKKKK (King KITTENS Krazy Kone Koncession). She pictured Fred getting a black raspberry marble ice cream cone. Even a single scoop would be a giant step for Fred.

Even if Fred just ate the ice cream and put the cone in his pocket "for later," that would make Betty so happy.

Even if Fred wanted a milk shake, that would be great.

Betty was mistaken.

Your Turn to Play

1. There are 87 flavors of ice cream at KKKKK. There are 6 different cones to choose among.

How many different ways could Fred build a single-scoop ice cream cone?

He would first have to pick one of the 87 flavors and then pick one of the 6 cones.

2. Betty and Alexander would each get a single scoop in a cup. They knew that they would be eating a big pizza dinner at PieOne and they didn't want to ruin their appetites.

Betty had a choice of 87 flavors and so did Alexander.

For example, Betty might choose black walnut, and Alexander might choose pineapple.

That would make the ordered pair (black walnut, pineapple) in which the first coordinate is Betty's choice and the second coordinate is Alexander's. How many ordered pairs are possible?

3. {yam} is the set of all flavors at KKKKK that begin with the letter Y. What is the cardinality of that set?

4. The first letter of the Greek alphabet is alpha (α). Make a guess of the cardinality of the set of all flavors at KKKKK that begin with α.

.... ANSWERS ....

1. If there are 87 ways to pick the flavor and 6 ways to pick the cone, then there are 87 × 6 ways to choose both.

$$\overset{4}{8}7$$
$$\underline{\times\ \ 6}$$
$$522$$ There are 522 possible combinations.

2. There are 87 possible choices for the first coordinate (Betty's choice of ice cream flavor). There are 87 possible choices for the second coordinate (Alexander's choice of ice cream flavor).

   Therefore, there are 87 × 87 possible ordered pairs.

$$87$$
$$\underline{\times 87}$$
$$609$$
$$\underline{696\ \ }$$
$$7569$$ There are 7,569 possible choices for them.

3. The cardinality of {yam} is one. The set has only one element in it.

4. All of the flavors at KKKKK are named using the Roman alphabet: ABCDEFGHIJKLMNOPQRSTUVWXYZ.

None of the flavors are written in the Greek alphabet: αβγδεζηθικλμνξοπρστυφχψω.

Here is the set of all flavors beginning with α: { }. This is called the empty set. Its cardinality is 0.

Chapter Nine
The Right Machine

Please do the honey cards.

Alexander had told Fred that he had two questions. He asked his second question, "Fred, you said that Polka Dot Publishing asked you to talk about any math or pizza topic. You said you are going to talk about ice cream."

Again, Alexander failed to make his question explicit,* but Fred knew what he was driving at.

Fred answered, "Everything is related to pizza and to math. I'll make the connection somehow. I haven't figured out how yet."

Betty was crestfallen (discouraged, dejected, distressed) when Fred led them right past the King KITTENS Krazy Kone Koncession. She said, "I thought we were going to King KITTENS to get some ice cream to eat."

Fred smiled and said, "We are going to get some ice cream."

Alert readers will have noticed that Fred left two words out of his reply . . . to eat.

---

* Explicit = clearly expressed. *Explicit* is the opposite of *implicit*.

Betty and Alexander followed silently behind as Fred dashed through the 21 acres of shopping at King KITTENS. (There were three main floors at King KITTENS, and each floor was seven acres.)

He rushed by the I-beam department. He wasn't going to do any building today.

He ran past the Iberian Peninsula maps.

A peninsula is land almost completely surrounded by water. (If it is completely surrounded by water, it's called an island.)

Iberia = Spain and Portugal. (i-BEER-ee-ah)

He didn't stop at the ibex (I-bix) statues.

ibex

A mountain goat with long horns that curve backward. They can't be found in Kansas since they live in Europe, Asia, and northern Africa.

These plastic statues are two inches (5 centimeters) tall.

Very few people in Kansas own more than two or three of them.

Alexander started to see a pattern: I-beam, Iberian, Ibex. Fred stopped when he came to . . .

ICE CREAM MACHINES

World's Largest Assortment

There were ones that you crank by hand.

 There were electric models.

There were ones that made only one scoop.

 There were industrial-size models that could supply the ice cream needs of the Iberian Peninsula in summertime.

Ice cream maker salesman

"Hi. Can I help you pick out the ice cream machine of your dreams?"

Fred knew he was at the right place.

Fred explained to the salesman that he was the keynote speaker at the Math and Pizza Conference at four o'clock this afternoon and that he needed an ice cream maker for his talk about ice cream.

The salesman looked at the clock and said, "It's a quarter after two right now. That's plenty of time to get you the perfect ice cream maker."

2:15 p.m.

He began asking questions so that Fred would get exactly the right machine.

From 2:15 to 3
    is 45 minutes.
From 3 to 4
    is one hour.
Fred had one hour and forty-five minutes before he would begin his speech.

1. Do you want a hand-crank or an electric model? (2 choices)

2. Do you want a red, a blue, a brown, a yellow, or a green model? (5 choices)

3. Do you want a machine with a wood exterior, a metal exterior, or one with a porcelain finish that looks like a bathtub? (3 choices)

4. Do you want one that serves one person, two people, five people, or 800 people? (4 choices)

5. Do you want one that uses rock salt and ice or do you want one that comes with its own refrigeration unit? (2 choices)

6. Do you want to take the machine with you or do you want us to deliver it by KITTENS campus mail? (2 choices)

It was now half past two. He had a lot of choices to make. Question one (hand-crank or electric) and the five colors of question two offered Fred ten possible machines. $2 \times 5 = 10$

2:30 p.m.

With the three possible exteriors (question three), he now had thirty possible machines. $2 \times 5 \times 3 = 10 \times 3 = 30$

Your Turn to Play

1. With all six questions, how many different possible ice cream makers were there?

$2 \times 5 \times 3 \times 4 \times 2 \times 2 = ?$

2. If it takes Fred 10 seconds to make each decision, how long will it take Fred to make the 6 decisions?

3. Some people are not as decisive as Fred. It takes them a lot longer to make a decision.

When asked whether they want a wood exterior, a metal exterior, or a porcelain finish, they wonder whether the wood will give them splinters, whether the metal will show fingerprints, and whether the porcelain will crack.

I can't make up my mind.

Suppose it takes 10 minutes to make each decision. How long would it take to make the 6 decisions?

........ANSWERS ....

1. $2 \times 5 \times 3 \times 4 \times 2 \times 2 =$
        $10 \times 3 \times 4 \times 2 \times 2 =$
        $30 \times 4 \times 2 \times 2 =$
        $120 \times 2 \times 2 =$
        $240 \times 2 =$
        480

There are 480 possible ways that Fred could answer those six questions.

2. If it takes 10 seconds to answer one question, it will take six times as long to answer six questions.

    $10 \times 6 = 60.$

It will take Fred 60 seconds to answer all six questions. Sixty seconds is the same as one minute.

3. If it takes 10 minutes to answer one question, it will take six times as long to answer six questions.

    $10 \times 6 = 60.$

It will take 60 minutes to answer all six questions. Sixty minutes is the same as one hour.

In the metric system you change units by multiplying or dividing by tens. For example, a hundred centimeters is a meter. A thousand meters is kilometer.

Except in the metric system . . . 60 seconds is still a minute and 60 minutes is still an hour.

Chapter Ten
Ingredients

Please do the honey cards.

In case you are curious, Fred chose an electric model, that was green with a metal finish, that served 800 people, and that came with its own refrigeration unit. He asked that it be delivered by KITTENS campus mail to the PieOne restaurant where he would be speaking at four.

"Since this is February in Kansas," the salesman said, "we have a special sale today on ice cream makers. The model you have selected is normally $300. You only have to pay half of that price."

That was an easy division:

$$
\begin{array}{r}
150 \\
2\overline{)\ 300} \\
\underline{2} \\
10 \\
\underline{10} \\
00 \\
\underline{0} \\
0
\end{array}
$$

Instead of $300, Fred only had to pay $150.

Since he started with the $400 honorarium, he now had $250.

$$
\begin{array}{r}
{\scriptstyle 3\ 10} \\
4\cancel{0}0 \\
-\ 150 \\
\hline
250
\end{array}
$$

Betty looked at Fred and wondered whether he would ever eat any of the ice cream that this machine would make.

Fred knew that an ice cream machine wouldn't make ice cream until you first put in the ingredients.

Fred turned to the salesman and asked, "What stuff do you stick in the machine?"

The salesman said that the ice cream recipe book is $6.

$$\begin{array}{r} 250 \\ -6 \\ \hline 244 \end{array}$$

Fred now had $244.

He opened to the first chapter and started reading. He announced to Betty and Alexander, "It looks like I have to buy a cow."

"What!" cried Alexander. "What are you reading?"

Fred proffered* him the book. Alexander turned to the first chapter.

Chapter One

If you want to make ice cream, the first thing you need is milk. This chapter will teach you how to milk your cow.

Alexander asked Fred, "Did you see when this book was written? In 1843, lots of people lived on farms and had cows. And they had no electric refrigerators."

"But how did they get ice?" Fred asked.

Alexander pointed to Chapter Two.

Chapter Two

If this is wintertime in Kansas, there is no problem finding ice. Just walk outside.

In the winter, chop blocks of ice out of the lake and store them in an ice house. Then you'll have ice in the summer.

---

* To proffer is to offer with hope of acceptance.

Betty said, "It's 2:30, and you have to present your speech in an hour and a half. Let's get to the grocery store and buy the stuff you need. This isn't the year 1843."

The grocery store was at the east end of King KITTENS. They had a five-minute walk to get to ABCDEFG.

As they walked, Fred turned to the recipe section of the book to find out what ingredients they would need to purchase.

Recipe for Making Ice Cream

For One Serving

8 oz. of fresh-squeezed cow (milk)

3 T of sugar

1 t vanilla

Fred knew what *oz.* meant. Since this was a liquid, it means fluid ounces. Since the recipe was in U.S. measurements instead of metric, he looked at Prof. Eldwood's Handy Chart in the back of the book:

60 drops = 1 t (teaspoon)	8 ounces = 1 cup
3 t = 1 T (tablespoon)	4 cups = 1 quart
2 T = 1 fluid ounce	4 quarts = 1 gallon

In the metric system, it's a little less complicated: 1000 milliliters = 1 liter

---

Your Turn to Play

1. Fred didn't want one serving. He needed 800 servings. Looking at the recipe for one serving (on the previous page), determine how many ounces of milk he will need.

2. How many cups will that be?

3. How many quarts will that be?

4. How many gallons will that be?

5. If a gallon of milk weighs about 8 pounds, how many pounds of milk will Fred, Alexander, and Betty have to carry?

6. They had walked to King KITTENS. It had been Betty's intention to get a black raspberry marble ice cream cone for Fred.

Given your answer to question 5, will Alexander have to go and get his car while Fred and Betty shop at ABCDEFG for the ice cream ingredients?

Choose one answer: ☐ Yes or ☐ Yes.

In case you are wondering, ABCDEFG stands for

All the Best
Coupon Depot
Extra Foody Groceries

·······ANSWERS·······

1. One serving required 8 oz. Eight hundred servings
will require 800 times as much.

$$\begin{array}{r} 800 \\ \times\ \ 8 \\ \hline 6400 \end{array}$$ They will need 6,400 ounces of milk.

2. There are 8 oz. in a cup. Do we add, subtract,
multiply, or divide? (You may have heard this before.)
When in doubt, restate the problem with simple
numbers.

   Suppose we had 16 ounces of milk. That would be 2
cups. We divided.

   So we divide 6,400 by 8.

$$\begin{array}{r} 800\ \ \ \ \ \\ 8{\overline{)\,6400}} \\ \underline{64}\ \ \ \ \ \end{array} \Rightarrow 800 \text{ cups}$$

   (I skipped putting in all the extra zeros in the
division. Some people like to write

$$\begin{array}{r} 800 \\ 8{\overline{)\,6400}} \\ \underline{64} \\ 00 \\ \underline{00} \\ 00 \\ \underline{00} \\ 0 \end{array}$$

but I figure it's a waste of time.
It's your choice.)

3. 800 cups (when there are 4 cups to the quart) . . .

   $800 \div 4 = 200$ quarts.

4. 200 quarts $\div 4 = 50$ gallons.

5. 50 gallons times 8 lbs. per gallon $= 400$ lbs.

6. ☒ Yes Carrying 400 lbs. would be hard to do.

Chapter Eleven
Seat Belts

Please do the honey cards. Any discomfort you feel is ignorance leaving your brain.

W hen Alexander rolled up to the front of ABCDEFG, Betty and Fred were waiting for him. They were pushing several shopping carts filled with 50 gallons of milk, several bags of sugar, and about a gallon of vanilla.

After they filled the car, there was one slight difficulty. There was no room for Fred.

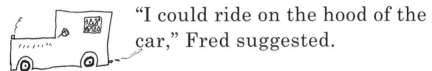

"I could ride on the hood of the car," Fred suggested.

"Then I couldn't see where I was driving," Alexander replied.

Fred hopped on top of the car and said, "Now I won't interfere with your driving."

Betty was frightened at the thought of Fred riding on the roof of Alexander's car. "You don't have a seat belt. What if you fall off?"

Alexander supplied Fred with a seat belt.

Alexander made a right turn and they realized that the seat belt wasn't going to work.

"I think we'll have to switch to Plan B," Alexander said.

"What's Plan B?" Betty asked.

"I'm not sure," Alexander answered. "I haven't thought of it yet."

Fred slipped out of the seat belt and said, "I'll race you. I'll jog and you drive. I'll meet you at PieOne."

It would be a short race.

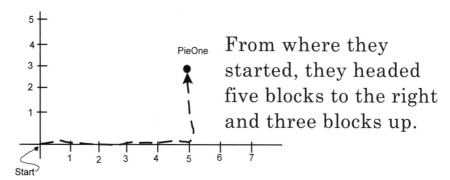

From where they started, they headed five blocks to the right and three blocks up.

The ordered pair (5, 3) tells where PieOne is located.

The first coordinate tells you how far to the right to go. The second coordinate tells you how far up. (☞, ♭)

Putting a point on a map is called graphing.

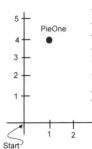

If the PieOne pizza place were located here, it would have coordinates (1, 4). From the start you would go to the right 1 block and then 4 blocks up.

Alexander and Betty arrived at PieOne a couple of minutes before Fred.

"You won!" said Fred.

"Yes, but we could use a little help," said Alexander. "We can't get out of the car."

Fred unbuckled the seat belt so that the doors could be opened.

People were already starting to arrive for the conference, and it wasn't even three o'clock yet. Lots of them helped Betty, Alexander, and Fred carry all the ingredients for the ice cream inside.

Fred remembered when he was four months old and saw the sampler that his mother had put on the wall.

A sampler is a piece of cloth with a saying stitched into it.

His mother had bought this sampler at a yard sale. She thought it was about the electric company. With a felt tip pen, she altered the sampler.

Many Hands Make the Lights work.

If Fred's mother could have seen how quickly the 50 gallons of milk, the bags of sugar, and the vanilla were carried into PieOne, she might have understood what "Many hands make light work" really meant.

Alexander had parked his car 6 yards from the front door of PieOne. If he had parked on the sidewalk, he would have been 2 yards and 2 feet closer to the front door.*

If he had parked on the sidewalk, how close to the front door would he be? Do we add, subtract, multiply, or divide? We restate the problem with simpler numbers. Suppose he would be 6 yards away if he parked on the street and he would be 1 yard closer if he parked on the sidewalk. Then he would be 5 yards from the door. We subtracted.

So we subtract 2 yards, 2 feet from 6 yards.

---

* He would have also gotten a parking ticket. You are supposed to park on the street and not on the sidewalk.

$$
\begin{array}{ll}
6 \text{ yards} \\
-2 \text{ yards} \quad 2 \text{ feet}
\end{array}
\quad \Longrightarrow \quad
\begin{array}{ll}
\overset{5}{\cancel{6}} \text{ yards} & 3 \text{ feet} \\
-2 \text{ yards} & 2 \text{ feet} \\
\hline
3 \text{ yards} & 1 \text{ foot}
\end{array}
$$

We borrowed one yard and that gave us 3 feet.

Your Turn to Play

1. Suppose you are 6 miles away from PieOne and you move 29 feet closer. How far away are you now?

(There are 5,280 feet in a mile.)

2. Suppose Fred weighed 37 pounds and he lost 3 ounces. How much would he weigh now?

(There are 16 ounces in a pound.)

3. Suppose a building is 15 meters tall. (A meter is a little longer than a yard.) If the building sank 8 centimeters into the ground, how tall would it now be?

(There are 100 centimeters in a meter.)

4. Suppose one of the gallons of milk leaked and lost 2 ounces. How much would remain?

(There are 128 fluid ounces in a gallon.)

. . . . ANSWERS . . . .

1.   6 miles

   $-$ 29 feet

   $\Rightarrow$

   $\overset{5}{6}$ miles   5280 feet

   $-$ 29 feet

   5 miles   5251 feet

2.   37 lbs.

   $-$ 3 oz.

   $\Rightarrow$

   $\overset{36}{37}$ lbs.   16 oz.

   $-$ 3 oz.

   36 lbs.   13 oz.

3.   15 m

   $-$ 8 cm

   $\Rightarrow$

   $\overset{14}{15}$ m   100 cm

   $-$ 8 cm

   14 m   92 cm

4.   1 gallon

   $-$ 2 oz.

   $\Rightarrow$

   $\overset{0}{1}$ gallon   128 oz.

   $-$ 2 oz.

   126 oz.

The abbreviations for pounds (lbs.) and for ounces (oz.) require periods.

The abbreviations for meters (m) and centimeters (cm) do not require periods.

Chapter Twelve
PieOne

Please do the honey cards. It only takes a minute or two.

Stanley Anthony greeted everyone as they entered his pizza place. Many students and faculty at KITTENS had been coming to PieOne for years. He knew them all by name.

"Welcome Fred! Welcome Betty! Welcome Alexander," he called out.

Stanley Anthony is a longer name—five syllables. Over the years some of the students started calling him Stananthony—four syllables. And then they shortened it to three syllables—Stanthony.*

He was happy with any of those names and used to say, "You can call me any of those names as long as you like my pizza."

When Stanthony was born, his name was Ed Lee. He was the great-great-great grandson of Robert E(dward) Lee, the general who

_____

* Some day they may shorten it to two syllables—Tony. Or even to one syllable—Stan. But that hasn't happened yet.

commanded the army of the Confederate States of America during the last three years of the Civil War. Years ago when Ed Lee started PieOne, he changed his name to Stanley Anthony Michelangelo di Lodovico Buonarroti Simoni. That sounded more Italian.

Ed had chosen *Stanley Anthony* because it rhymed. He had taken the rest of his name, *Michelangelo di Lodovico Buonarroti Simoni,* out of the encyclopedia.[*]

Stanthony told Fred, "Your big green machine was delivered this afternoon. It fit perfectly in the alcove in the back of the building."

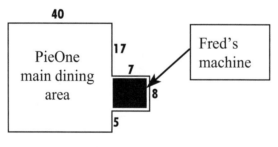

Map of PieOne

Stanthony showed Fred a map of the building that included the alcove.

---

[*] Michelangelo di Lodovico Buonarroti Simoni is the artist who painted the ceiling of the Sistine Chapel. He is often referred to as Michelangelo. His mother may have shortened that to Mike.

"That's a beautiful green machine," Stanthony said. "I only have one question. What is it?"

Fred explained that it was an ice cream maker and he would use it in his talk at the Math and Pizza Conference this afternoon.

"But it's so big!"

Fred explained that it was one of the larger models.

"But why is it green?"

Fred said that he had had choice of five colors—red, blue, brown, yellow, or green—and he had picked green since it was the color of the grass that cows ate.

"How does it work?"

Fred had a simple answer for that question. "I'm not sure. I've never made ice cream before."

"I have only one last question. I'm thinking of stringing a line of Christmas lights around the outside of PieOne. I need the perimeter of the building so I can order the right length. The map is missing some numbers. Would you come with me outside and hold one end of my tape measure?"

Christmas lights? Fred thought to himself. *This is February. Aren't we rushing things a little bit?*

Fred looked at the map.

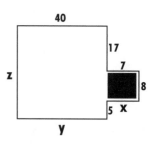

There were three distances that were unknown. Fred labeled them x, y, and z. (In algebra, x, y, and z are often the letters used for unknowns.)

Fred would have been happy to help Stanthony do the measuring, but there was an easier way. Thought could replace physical effort.

He knew that x would have to be 7. They were opposite sides of a rectangle.

He knew that y would have to be 40 for the same reason.

Finding z was a little harder. For a moment, Fred looked at three numbers on the map.

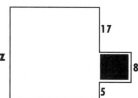

If he added up 17 + 8 + 5, that would equal the length of the right side of the big rectangle.

So z = 17 + 8 + 5, which is 30.

small essay
Why Math?

Mathematics was invented for one reason: to save work. It's that simple. Fred used math to find the values of x, y, and z. He didn't have to go outside and do the measurements.

If you have 23 cows in the west field and 18 cows in the east field, you could find out how many cows you owned by counting them: 1, 2, 3, 4, 5, 6, 7, 8, 9, 10, 11, . . . , 39, 40, 41. Or you could use addition and get the answer with much less effort: 23 + 18 = 41. Addition makes your life easier.

Your Turn to Play

1. Suppose you were two years old and had 7 boxes of chocolate drops and each box contained three chocolate drops. If you wanted to find out how many drops you owned, you would break open all the boxes and start counting.

$1\,2^3\ 4\,5^6\ 7\,8^9\ \ 10\,11^{12}\ \ 13\,14^{15}\ \ 16\,17^{18}\ \ 19\,20^{21}$

If you were four years old and knew a little more math, you would use addition to make your work easier. 3 + 3 + 3 + 3 + 3 + 3 + 3 = 21

Now you are older. What math will make this even easier?

2. What is the perimeter of the PieOne building?

3. Stanthony wants to install new carpet. What is the area of the floor in the PieOne building? (The area of a rectangle is length times width.)

. . . . ANSWERS . . . .

1. Counting: $1$$2^3$ $4$$5^6$ $7$$8^9$ $10$$11^{12}$ $13$$14^{15}$ $16$$17^{18}$ $19$$20^{21}$

   Adding: $3 + 3 + 3 + 3 + 3 + 3 + 3 = 21$

   Multiplying: $7 \times 3 = 21$

Math was created to make our lives easier.*

2.

We add up all the lengths:

$$
\begin{array}{r}
30 \\
40 \\
17 \\
7 \\
8 \\
7 \\
5 \\
+\ 40 \\
\hline
154
\end{array}
$$

The perimeter is 154 feet.

3. The area of the larger rectangle is $30 \times 40 = 1200$.

The area of the small rectangle is $7 \times 8 = 56$.

$$
\begin{array}{r}
40 \\
\times\ 30 \\
\hline
00 \\
120 \\
\hline
1200
\end{array}
$$

$$1200 + 56 = 1256$$

The total area is 1256 square feet.

---

* On the other hand, math taught poorly can be torture. Hours of drill, drill, drill reminds me of going to the dentist.

   Ice cream eating taught poorly can be torture. First, the teacher makes you swim in icy water for an hour until your teeth are chattering. Then you are forced to eat a gallon of avocado ice cream.

Chapter Thirteen
Before Four

Please do the honey cards. Are you getting faster than when you first used the honey cards?

F red looked at the clock. He had 55 minutes until the Math and Pizza Conference would begin. Already, fifty people had arrived for the meeting.

Some of the people were Fred's students. Darlene and Joe were there. Joe was always early when food was involved.

3:05 p.m.

Fred introduced himself to some of the people he didn't know. There was a couple who were math professors at one of the big California universities. They had brought their three little kids with them. She invited Fred to sit with them.

She said, "Then you could have someone to play with during the keynote speech."

Fred hadn't mentioned that he was the keynote speaker. All he had mentioned was his name and that he was five years old. He didn't want people to think that he was only four.

There were math teachers from Germany, France, and Poland.

A woman who was a famous pizza chef came from Italy. She told Fred that she had come to learn why Stanley Anthony's pizza was world-famous. Fred introduced her to Stanthony. She spoke to him in Italian thinking, *With a name like Stanley Anthony Michelangelo di Lodovico Buonarroti Simoni he must have grown up in Italy.*

He didn't understand a word she said.

Fred wandered back through the crowd. It was getting noisy at PieOne. There were lively conversations about category theory, linear functionals, homeomorphisms, and other math topics.

Kids were running around.

A television set mounted on the wall was showing a Marx Brothers' movie in which Chico Marx spoke with an Italian accent. Stanthony thought this made PieOne more authentically Italian.

Fred needed a place to be alone for a moment before his speech. He looked at the big green machine in the alcove. He climbed up the front of the machine and sat on top.

He could look down over the crowd. This made him feel very tall.

Am I forgetting anything? Fred wondered.

✓ His pink bow tie was straight.

✓ His brown shoes were polished.

✓ He had all the ingredients for making ice cream.

There were only two minor* things that Fred had forgotten: ① He didn't know how to operate the ice cream maker and ② he hadn't prepared his speech.

Fred spotted a little booklet taped to the top of the ice cream maker.

If he hadn't climbed on top of the big green machine, he would never have found the manual.

Instruction Manual

Ice Cream Maker

Prof. Eldwood

Step One: Plug it in.

Fred climbed down and found the electric cord.

I bet this will take lots of electricity.

Step Two: Pull down on the Freezing Lever to set coldness.

Warning: Lever is on a spring. Press harder to make it colder.

---

* This is irony (Eye-ron-knee). Irony is saying the opposite of what you really mean with the knowledge that both speaker and listener know what you're doing.

Those two items that Fred had forgotten were major items, not minor ones.

You are speaking ironically if you call Fred a heavyweight, or say that the oceans are just a couple of drops of water.

Fred wasn't sure what this meant until he looked at the lever.

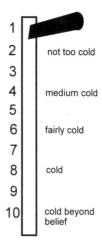

He pulled down on the lever with one pound of force. The lever moved to 3.

When he pulled down with three pounds of force, the lever moved to 6.

Fred didn't want to overdo it. He figured that moving the lever to 9 would be perfect. He had two pieces of information: One pound moved the lever to 3 and three pounds moved the lever to 6. Two ordered pairs: (1, 3) and (3, 6).

He graphed those two points.

To graph (1, 3), you go over 1 and up 3.

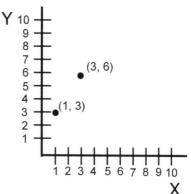

To graph (3, 6), you go over 3 and up 6.

In the ordered pair (x, y), the x was the pounds that he applied to the lever, and the y was the position to which the lever moved.

Fred drew a line through the two points. (Small intermission.

Fred had studied high school physics and knew about Hooke's law: *How far a spring stretches is proportional to how hard you pull on it.* Translation: When you graph pull vs. displacement, it will be a straight line. The instruction manual had said that the lever was on a spring.)

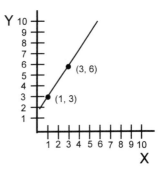

Your Turn to Play

1. Here's the fun part. Tell by just looking at the graph how many pounds Fred would have to pull on the lever to make it move to 9.

No adding, subtracting, multiplying, or dividing! Some students really love graphing.

2. [Question for art majors] On a piece of paper graph (2, 5), (4, 3), and (8, 1). Are those three points on a straight line?

3. Recall (from *Life of Fred: Honey*) that the slope of a line is defined as $\dfrac{\text{rise}}{\text{run}}$

Slope = the rise divided by the run.

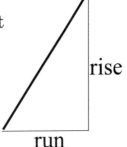

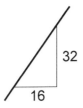

What is the slope of this line?

· · · · · · ·ANSWERS· · · · · · ·

1.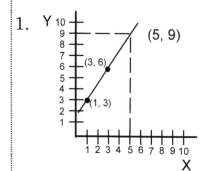

We want to find out what number of pounds corresponds to 9 on the lever.

Restated: We want to find out what point on the line corresponds to (?, 9).

It looks like if Fred pulls down on the lever with 5 pounds of force, the lever will move to 9.

2. Those three points are not collinear (on the same line).

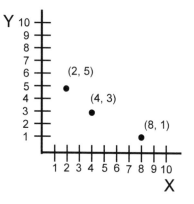

3.

The slope is equal to $\dfrac{32}{16}$ which can be written as $32 \div 16$

or as $16\overline{)32}$

Doing the division we have:

$$16\overline{)\begin{array}{r} 2 \\ 32 \end{array}}$$
$$\underline{32}$$
$$0$$

The slope is equal to 2.

Chapter Fourteen
Starting the Machine

Please do the honey cards. Some day you will be able to do them all without a single mistake.

F red pulled down with five pounds of force and the lever moved to 9. The ice cream maker rumbled as the refrigeration unit turned on. Fred continued reading.

1
2   not too cold
3
4   medium cold
5
6   fairly cold
7
8   cold
9
10 cold beyond belief

Step Three: Pour in all the ingredients and flip on the Stir Switch.

Since this involved food, Joe was standing there watching what was happening. Fred asked Joe to help pour in the 50 gallons of milk, the bags of sugar, and the gallon of vanilla. Joe was glad to help.

Fred started to search for the stir switch. The front panel was filled with dials and gauges but no switches.

Front Panel

The side of the ice cream maker just had the serial number plate.

Model 396263XLM39–559–B
Serial Number: 566878956489413138515634488646000028.45466

Fred always wondered why serial numbers were so long. Had the manufacturers made *that* many machines?

In the back of the ice cream maker, five cm (that's about two inches) from the floor, was a tiny switch marked Stir. Fred flipped it on.

The ground shook as the machine began to stir the ingredients.

Step Four: Wait. When the bells ring and the lights flash, the ice cream will be ready.

Handy Chart (for lever set at 9)	
If you are making ice cream for . . .	Done in . . .
40 people	3 minutes
280 people	21 minutes

What! thought Fred. *This is a silly chart. It's so small. The machine is supposed to make ice cream for up to 800 people. Why doesn't the chart list 800 people?*

It was now 40 minutes until four o'clock. He needed to know when the ice cream was going to be done. It would make a big difference if bells rang and lights flashed in the

3:20

middle of his speech or at ten o'clock at night after everyone had gone home.

The handy chart gave Fred two data points: (40 people, 3 minutes) and (280 people, 21 minutes).

The first coordinate (also known as the x-coordinate) was the number of people.

The second coordinate (also known as the y-coordinate) was the time it took to make the ice cream.

If Fred tried to plot the point (280, 21) on a graph that looked like this he would need a huge sheet of paper.

Instead, he changed the scale on the graph. He needed the first coordinate (the x-coordinate) to be at least 800, because he wanted to find out how long it would take to make the ice cream for 800 people.

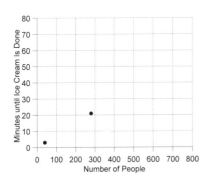

He plotted the points (40, 3) and (280, 21).

Plotting is a little like art. You have to sometimes estimate where you are going to put the dot.

To plot (40, 3), Fred knew that 40 was not quite half way to 100 and that 3 is about one-third of the way to 10.

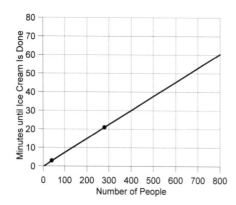

He drew a line through the two points.

The original chart that came in the instructional manual only mentioned 40 people and 280 people. The line on this graph tells how long it will take to make the ice cream *for any number of people.*

Fred wanted to know how long it would take for 800 people. The point on the line is (800, 60). In sixty minutes the ice cream would be done.

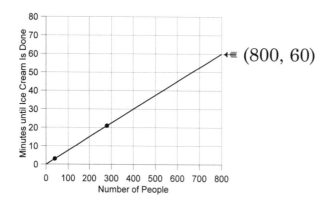

Scientists and engineers use graphs all the time to make estimations. They plot the points that they know, they draw the line, and then they can make their predictions.

Your Turn to Play

1. Look at the graph on the previous page. How long would the machine take to make ice cream for 400 people?

2. Looking at that graph, estimate how long it would take to make ice cream for 600 people.

3. The graph on the previous page illustrates a function. The domain is the number of people. What is the codomain?

4. Suppose you manufactured televisions and put a serial number on each set. Your first set would be

| Serial Number: 1 |

How many digits would your largest serial number be if you sold a set to each person in the United States?

(The current population is about three hundred million.)

5. You and 26 of your friends worked together to make those televisions. After paying for the materials and paying the taxes, the final profits were $1,026. How much would each of you (there are 27 of you) receive?

6. If you could carve one horse statue in 2 hours and 9 statues in 6 hours, how long would it take to carve 3 statues? (Big hint: Plot the points (1, 2) and (9, 6). Draw a straight line through those two points. Estimate what y would be if x were 3.)

·······ANSWERS·······

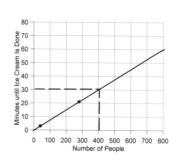

1. The point (400, 30) is on the line.

2. When the x value (the number of people) is 600, it looks like the y value (the minutes until the ice cream is done) is about half way between 40 and 50.

    I estimate (600, 45). It will take about 45 minutes.

3. The codomain is the number of minutes until the ice cream is done.

4. Your last serial number will be about 300,000,000. You will need 9 digits.

5. We want $1,026 to be divided equally into 27 parts.

$$\begin{array}{r} 38 \\ 27\overline{)1026} \\ \underline{81} \\ 216 \\ \underline{216} \\ 0 \end{array}$$ Each would receive $38.

6. For three statues carved it appears that it will take approximately 3 hours.

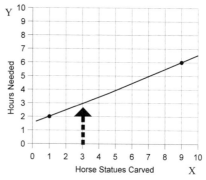

Chapter Fifteen
Booths at the Conference

Please do the honey cards.

It was 3:20. The ice cream would be ready in 60 minutes. The bells would ring and the lights would flash at 4:20.

Since Fred would start speaking at 4:00, he would speak for 20 minutes before The Great Event (= the ice cream).

By now, over a hundred people had arrived at PieOne for the Math and Pizza Conference.

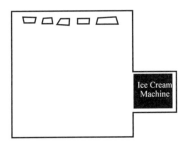

On the north side of the room, people had set up booths to sell things at the conference.

One of the most popular was the Pizza Button booth. Almost everyone stopped and bought some of them.

Joe bought one of them. He was going to use it to bait his hook when he went fishing. He paid a dime and got a penny in change.

Darlene bought 10 of them. That cost 90 cents (10 × 9¢). She paid a dollar and got a dime in change (90¢ + 10¢ = $1). She was going to sew them on her wedding dress. She had been thinking of marrying Joe for years, but hadn't told him yet.

Fred bought 7 Pizza Buttons and paid a dollar. He liked the way the buttons smelled. That was a 63-cent purchase (7 × 9¢). That part was easy for anyone who knows the nine-times table.

There are three ways to figure out how much change Fred should get.

Way #1: You get out a piece of paper and do the subtraction:

$$
\begin{array}{r}
100¢ \\
-\ \ 63¢ \\
\hline
37¢
\end{array}
$$

Way #2: You punch into your calculator ⌶ ◫ ◫ - ㄅ Ꝑ = and the display reads Ꝑ Ꝑ.

Way #3: You learn how to **count back the change**. This is the easiest way and probably the fastest.

You start with the amount of the purchase 63¢.
You give the buyer two pennies

and say **64, 65**.

You give a dime   and say **75**.

You give a quarter   and say **one dollar**.

Stanthony bought 8 Pizza Buttons and paid a dollar. The amount of the purchase was 72¢ (8 × 9¢).

Start with purchase price of 72¢.
You give the buyer three pennies

and say **73, 74, 75.**

You give a quarter   and say **one dollar.**

Alexander bought 2 Pizza Buttons and paid a dollar.

Purchase price was 18¢ (2 × 9¢).
You give the buyer two pennies

and say **19, 20.**

You give the buyer a nickel   and say **25.**

You give the buyer three quarters

and say **50, 75, one dollar.**

18 → 19 → 20 → 25 → 50 → 75 → one dollar.

Betty bought 3 Pizza Buttons and paid a dollar. $3 \times 9¢$

27 → 28 → 29 → 30 → 40 → 50 → 75 →one dollar

Time Out!

The best way to practice counting back change is to actually do it.

What you need are 4 pennies, 1 nickel, 2 dimes, and 3 quarters.

Then you can make change for any purchase up to a dollar.

Have your mother/father/brother/sister/grandmother/dentist/butler name a purchase amount such as 93¢, and you count back the change: 93 → 94 → 95 → one dollar.

Every coin has "IN GOD WE TRUST" on it.

Every coin has "LIBERTY" on it. Liberty is not the same as freedom. Liberty means a special kind of freedom—freedom for the rights of individuals over the power of the state.

Your Turn to Play

1. Assume you are paid a dollar for an 85¢ purchase. You would count back 85 ➔ **90** ➔ **one dollar**.

Do this now for each of the following purchases:

23¢ ➔ . . .

55¢ ➔ . . .

3¢ ➔ . . .

2. We used "∪" to indicate the union of two sets.

   Is ∪ commutative?

3. $6^2 = ?$

4. Sam fell in love with Pizza Buttons and bought $6.84 of them. (That's the same as 684¢.) They sell for 9¢ each. How many did he buy?

.......**ANSWERS**.......

1.   23¢ → 24 → 25 → 50 → 75 → one dollar

55¢ → 65 → 75 → one dollar

3¢ → 4 → 5 → 15 → 25 → 50 → 75 → one dollar

2. Does {A, B} ∪ {B, 4, ✐} give the same answer as {B, 4, ✐} ∪ {A, B}? Yes.

They are both equal to {A, B, 4, ✐}. The order in which you list the elements of a set does not matter. {A, B, 4, ✐} is the same set as {✐, A, 4, B}.

∪ is a commutative operation.

3. $6^2 = 6 \times 6 = 36$.

4. Total purchase of 684¢. Each one cost 9¢.

Do we add, subtract, multiply, or divide? When you are not sure, restate the problem with simple numbers. Suppose your purchase was 6¢ and they cost 2¢ each. Then you bought 3 of them. $6 \div 2 = 3$. Division.

$$\begin{array}{r} 76 \\ \hline 9)\overline{684} \\ \underline{63} \\ 54 \\ \underline{54} \end{array}$$

Sam bought 76 Pizza Buttons.

<u>A Row of Practice.</u> *Do the whole row before you look at the answers.*

84	347	53	698	749
+ 48	− 9	× 6	× 4	+ 962
132	338	318	2792	1711

Chapter Sixteen
Fast Freeze

Learning the times table is the last big memorization task that you will have in the whole Life of Fred series. Please do the honey cards.

After buying his Pizza Button, Joe wandered back to the ice cream machine. He couldn't wait for the ice cream to be done.

He briefly looked at all the dials and gauges but couldn't understand them.

Front Panel

Then he spotted the freezing lever. He had seen Fred pull down on that lever with five pounds of force. He thought to himself: *The colder the setting, the faster the machine will make ice cream.*

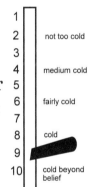

Joe put his hand on the lever, thought for a moment, and pulled it down to 10. The machine rumbled a little louder.

Joe put his elbow on the lever to add a little extra pressure. The lever stayed at 10.

Just for fun, Joe hopped up and sat on the lever. Here are two inequalities:

Joe's weight > 100 pounds.

Joe's IQ < 100.

```
1
2   not too cold
3
4   medium cold
5
6   fairly cold
7
8   cold
9
10  cold beyond
    belief
11
12
13
14
15
16
17
18
19
20
21
22
23
24
```

The handle broke off. Joe couldn't pull it back up to 9.

The lights in the PieOne building dimmed. The ice cream machine was using more electricity than all of KITTENS University normally uses.

But Joe was right about one thing: the ice cream would freeze a lot faster.

How fast? The bells on the machine were ringing and the lights were flashing. The ice cream was ready.

Alexander ran over to the machine. The lever was broken and couldn't be moved. The bells kept ringing. He unplugged the machine.

It was quiet. Everyone in the room was looking at Alexander, Joe, and the machine.

After a moment, Alexander announced, "The ice cream is ready a little earlier than we thought. If everyone would get a bowl and a spoon from Stanthony, we can begin the Math and Pizza Conference with dessert."

Eight hundred people were expected for the conference, but it was still early. There were only 200 here when the ice cream was passed out. Each person got four times as much.

$$200\overline{)800} \atop \underline{800}$$ with quotient 4

Six Things that Need to be Explained

1. How did they get the ice cream out of the machine if it was unplugged?

Alexander couldn't plug in the machine, otherwise the machine would continue to freeze and the bells would continue to ring. Instead, he took off a top panel, reached down, and scooped out the ice cream.

2. How much ice cream did each person get?

The original recipe (from Prof. Eldwood's *Making Ice Cream the Modern Way*) was: For One Serving—8 oz. of fresh-squeezed cow (milk). Since eight ounces is equal to a cup, each person received four cups of ice cream. That's one quart for each person.

3. How would these people be able to eat any of Stanthony's pizza if they had a quart of ice cream first?

They might not. But there were going to be 600 people (800 − 200), who didn't have any ice cream to spoil their dinner.

4. How can you make ice *cream* from fresh-squeezed cow (milk)? Was Prof. Eldwood wrong?

He was wrong. He had left out a step in the process. When a cow offers you some of her milk (only female animals give milk) part of it is cream and part of it is skim (non-fat) milk. A glass of fresh milk will have thick cream at the top and thinner skim milk at the bottom.

The milk that you buy at the store has been **homogenized**. It says so right on the carton. The cream and the skim milk have been scrambled up* so that the cream doesn't float to the top.

Prof. Eldwood should have written *cream* instead of *milk*.

5. How did the lever scale that only went to 10 suddenly go to 24?

Originally, this machine wasn't an ice cream machine. You can't go to a regular store in Kansas and purchase an ice cream maker for

---

* If I mentioned that the fat particles in the cream are emulsified, then I would have to explain what *emulsified* means. Then I would have to describe the process of suspending one liquid within another to create an emulsion.

Then I would have to explain why some liquids, like water, don't get along with other liquids, like oil or grease.

Did you ever notice that plain water won't wash grease off your hands?

Now you know why we use soap.

800 people. This particular machine was used in a science lab to study cryogenics (CRY-oh-gen-iks)—the study of super-low temperatures. Cryogenics goes far beyond refrigeration that's needed to make ice cream.* When they sold it as an ice cream maker, they covered over part of the scale on the lever.

Your Turn to Play

1. We'll let you explain the sixth thing that needs explaining.

Here is another page from the instruction manual:

Handy Chart (for serving 800 people)

Lever at . . .	Ice cream done in . . .
3	84 minutes
6	72 minutes

You have two points: (3, 84) and (6, 72). Plot them and estimate on your graph how long it would take to make the ice cream with the lever at 24.

---

* How cold? In cryogenics labs they turn air into a liquid!

Later on in your science studies we'll mention the use of adiabatic expansion for the liquefaction of gases such as helium and the truly weird properties that these super-cold liquids have.

I know—you can't wait. Here's one weird property. Helium doesn't become a mere liquid. It becomes a **superfluid**. It flows without any friction. Stir a cup of coffee and after a couple of minutes it will stop moving. Superfluid helium doesn't stop moving—even years later.

·······ANSWERS·······

1. When you do a graph, you will need a pencil, a piece of paper, and a ruler. Your work might look something like:

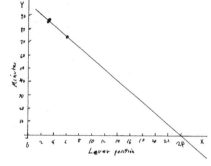

It looks like if the lever is at 24, it will take zero minutes to make the ice cream. This was, in fact, the case.

 If you had tons of casual cash, then you could have your butler go out to the store and buy graph paper for you.

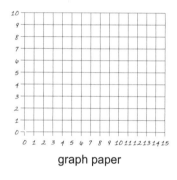

graph paper

It is paper with little squares on it. Then your graphs would be neater than the one at the top of this page. You wouldn't be any smarter—just neater.

On the other hand . . . if you were being paid big dollars to draw graphs, then you would get the fanciest graph paper and use the sharpest pencils. Your graph might look like this:

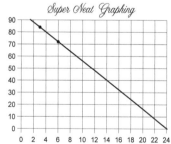

Super Neat Graphing

Chapter Seventeen
Joe and Ice Cream

Please do the honey cards.

Betty handed Fred a serving (one quart) of ice cream. She was hoping that he might eat a little bit of it. The protein in the milk would help build muscles, and the calcium will help his bones grow.

Fred thanked her and set the bowl on a table. There were only three times that Fred didn't eat: before giving a speech, during the speech, or afterwards.

Joe had finished his bowl of ice cream and pointed to Fred's bowl. "Are you going to eat that?"

Fred shook his head and said, "Be my guest."

Joe sat down at the table. At each table was a jar of honey. This was one of Stanthony's special treats for customers that had helped make PieOne world-famous. Some customers liked to put honey on their pizzas.

Joe poured half of the jar of honey on his ice cream, saying, "This needs a little sweetening."

Luckily, no one was listening to him. Watching Joe eat can make a normal person sick.

Darlene had only eaten three ounces of her bowl. She gave the rest to Joe.

$$
\begin{array}{r}
1 \text{ quart} \\
-\qquad\quad 3 \text{ ounces} \\
\hline
\end{array}
\qquad\qquad
\begin{array}{r}
\overset{0}{1} \text{ quart}\quad 32 \text{ ounces} \\
-\qquad\qquad\quad 3 \text{ ounces} \\
\hline
29 \text{ ounces}
\end{array}
$$

Joe emptied the other half of the jar of honey on Darlene's bowl.

Joe got half way through the 29 ounces of ice cream that Darlene had given him.

$$
\begin{array}{r}
14 \text{ R } 1 \\
2{\overline{)}\,29} \\
\underline{2} \\
9 \\
\underline{8} \\
1
\end{array}
$$

You really can't say that Joe ate 14 remainder 1 ounces.[*]

Instead, we can express the remainder as a fraction. We write $\dfrac{1}{2}$ instead of R 1.

The Rule: $\dfrac{\text{Remainder}}{\text{Divisor}}$

---

[*] Actually, you *can* say it but it doesn't make any sense.

Here are a ton of examples.

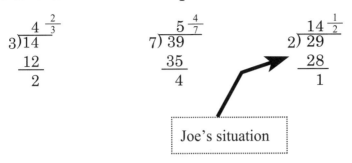

Joe's situation

Joe had eaten his own bowl (1 quart = 32 ounces). He had finished off Fred's bowl (1 quart). He was half way through Darlene's bowl (14 $\frac{1}{2}$ ounces).

small essay

Does Joe's Stomach Have Infinite Capacity?

Nothing in the physical world is infinite. If you can touch it, taste it, smell it, hear it, or see it, it is physical and finite.

Then is everything finite? No. Here are two examples of infinite: {1, 2, 3, 4, 5, . . . } and God.

end of small essay

No one had ever seen Joe stop eating. Joe could sit in front of his television and eat and eat and eat and eat. Waffles, potato chips, cake, cookies, candy bars—it didn't matter—Joe would eat it.

Today, Joe stopped eating. His eyeballs had turned blue from the cold of that much ice cream. His face turned greenish-orange. He had overdone it.

He stood up and walked quickly outside and regurgitated. Five minutes later he came back inside but didn't sit at the table where $14\frac{1}{2}$ ounces of uneaten ice cream were waiting for him.

$$14\frac{1}{2} \text{ ounces of Darlene's eaten}$$
$$+\ 14\frac{1}{2} \text{ ounces that Joe hadn't eaten}$$
$$\overline{28 + 1}$$

$$= 29 \text{ ounces Darlene gave him}$$

Joe was very quiet. He felt cold.

It was now twenty minutes to four. Alexander had finished scooping out the quarts of ice cream for the 200 people.

3:40 p.m.

He put the top panel back on the big green ice cream machine.

The machine was a mess. The handle on the lever was broken. There were gobs of ice cream on the front face of the machine, and the tub on the inside that had held the 50 gallons of milk needed to be washed.

Alexander got a big gray sheet and covered the machine so that it wouldn't be an eyesore.

Your Turn to Play

1. Fred looked at one of the booths on the north side of PieOne. This was new to him. Fred knew that braces were used to list the elements of a set. {❀, ©, ☎}

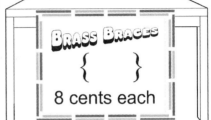

Fred asked, "Why would someone want braces made out of brass?"

He was told that brass braces would last a lot longer than regular braces.

Fred bought 8 of them and paid a dollar. Count back the change Fred would receive.

2. Darlene bought 9 of them and paid a dollar. Count back the change.

3. Joe wanted to use these brass braces as weights for his fishing lines. How many braces could he buy with a $10 bill (that's 1,000¢)?

4. How much would 100 braces cost?

5. The sheet that Alexander used to cover the ice cream machine was 9 feet long and 7 feet wide. What was the area of that sheet?

Hint: In algebra the area of a rectangle is given by the formula $A = \ell w$.

·······ANSWERS·······

1. If Fred bought 8 brass braces at 8¢ each, the purchase price would be 64¢. Counting back the change: 64 ➜ **65** ➜ **75** ➜ **one dollar.**

2. Nine braces at 8¢ each would cost 72¢. Counting back the change: 72 ➜ **73** ➜ **74** ➜ **75** ➜ **one dollar.**

3. We want to know how many 8¢ braces you can buy with 1,000¢. When you don't know whether to add, subtract, multiply, or divide, restate the problem with easier numbers.

   Suppose I wanted to know how many 8¢ braces I could buy with 24¢. The answer would be 3. I divided 8 into 24.

   Now, using the original numbers:

$$\begin{array}{r} 125 \\ 8\overline{)1000} \\ \underline{8} \\ 20 \\ \underline{16} \\ 40 \\ \underline{40} \end{array}$$

   He could buy 125 braces.

4. To multiply by 100, you add two zeros.
   8¢ × 100 = 800¢ which is $8.

5. A = ℓw = 9 × 7 = 63 square feet.

Chapter Eighteen
Fred Orders a Pizza

   Please do the honey cards. <u>This is the last time I</u>
<u>will ask you to use those cards</u>. If you have been
faithful in doing them, you should be able to graduate
from them at this point.

   Some students will continue to practice with
them at the beginning of future chapters, but that is
entirely their choice.

T hose brass braces each weighed five
ounces. Fred had bought eight of them.
Forty[*] ounces is the same as two pounds,
eight ounces.

$$\begin{array}{r} 2\ \text{R}\ 8 \\ 16\overline{)40} \\ \underline{32} \\ 8 \end{array}$$

1 lb. = 16 oz.

   It was getting close to four o'clock, and all
800 people had arrived for the Math and Pizza
Conference. No one wanted to be late and miss
a minute of the conference proceedings.

   Stanthony was running around taking
pizza orders. He didn't want to interrupt Fred's
speech. While Fred was talking, he could be in
the kitchen making all the pizzas.

---

[*] Have you ever noticed that there is no *u* in *forty*?

If a person wanted a one-topping pizza, Stanthony asked three questions:

① Which topping would you like? There were 49 possible choices.

② Which crust would you like? There were four choices: regular, thin, extra-thick, and whole wheat.

③ Do you want extra cheese?

There were 49 × 4 × 2 different one-topping pizzas possible.

If you wanted a rough estimate of how many that would be, you might compute 50 × 4 × 2, which is 200 × 2, which is 400. We know that the real answer would be a little less than that.

Of course, the people at the conference could order two toppings, or three toppings, or 49 toppings. They could order double extra cheese. For those with wheat allergies, they could order pizza without a crust.

When Stanthony came to Fred and asked what kind of pizza he would like, Fred said he wasn't very hungry.

Stanthony insisted, "You've got to order a pizza. We can make it an extra small,* just for you."

Fred was trapped. He asked Stanthony for the order pad and filled it out. Here's what Fred wrote.

PieOne

Topping(s) ___*no toppings please*___

Crust ___*skip the crust (Atkins' diet)*___

Extra cheese ___*make that no cheese*___

Special instructions ___*no sauce please*___

Size ___*extra-small (12-inch diameter)*___

---

* At PieOne, an extra-small is a 12-inch pizza. A regular is 18 inches.

His one-topping pizzas are usually about two inches (5 cm) thick. It is very difficult to leave PieOne and still be hungry.

When Fred handed the order pad back, Stanthony looked at it, frowned, and said, "There's not a single calorie here! A mouse couldn't live on that."

Fred took the order pad and made one change: Size ___**hungry-man (48-inch diameter)**___

After Stanthony got the pizza orders from everyone, he rushed into the kitchen to make 800 pizzas. The PieOne kitchen is in the backyard.

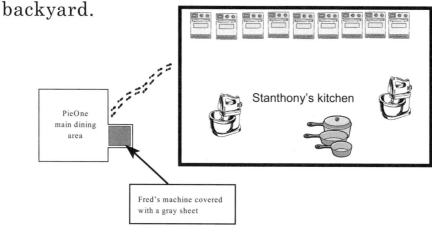

His kitchen is much larger than the dining area. He had nine giant pizza ovens on the north side of his kitchen. Earlier in the day he had rolled out most of the crusts. About an hour ago he had turned on all the ovens.

Yesterday, he had chopped up all the mushrooms, opened the cans of anchovies, diced the tomatoes, counted the pepperoni slices, grated the cheese, mashed the garlic, fried the hamburger, crumbled the bacon, stirred the sauce—in short, Stanthony was really ready to make a lot of pizzas quickly.

Your Turn to Play

1. It took Stanthony 4 seconds to make a pizza. How many seconds would it take to make 800 pizzas?

2. How many minutes and seconds would that be? Hint: Look at the beginning of this chapter when we converted forty ounces into pounds and ounces.

3. There are very few people who can make pizzas at the rate of one every four seconds.

Stanthony went to Robot Rentals and rented 19 pizza-making robots. They did the actual work of making the pizzas.

He rented the 19 robots for one hour. How much did that cost him?

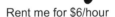

Rent me for $6/hour

4. A regular (18") six-topping pizza on extra thick crust is 287¢. (When you learn about decimals, we will write 287¢ as $2.87, but, for now, we'll just call it 287¢.)

How much would 18 of these pizzas cost?

· · · · · · · ANSWERS · · · · · · ·

1. We know that it takes 4 seconds to make a pizza, and we want to find out how long it would take to make 800 pizzas.

If you don't know whether to add, subtract, multiply, or divide, restate the problem with simple numbers and see which operation you use.

If it takes 4 seconds to make a pizza, how long would it take to make 3 pizzas? That would be 12 seconds. We multiplied.

In the original problem we multiply 4 times 800.

$$\begin{array}{r} 800 \\ \times\ \ 4 \\ \hline 3200 \end{array}$$ It would take 3,200 seconds.

2. We want to convert 3,200 seconds into minutes and seconds. Restating the problem with simple numbers, to convert 60 seconds into minutes you divide by 60.

We divide 3,200 by 60.

3,200 seconds =
53 minutes, 20 seconds

$$\begin{array}{r} 53\ \text{R}\ 20 \\ 60\overline{)\ 3200} \\ \underline{300} \\ 200 \\ \underline{180} \\ 20 \end{array}$$

3. 19 robots at \$6 per hour = 19 × 6

will cost \$114.

$$\begin{array}{r} \overset{5}{1}9 \\ \times\ \ 6 \\ \hline 114 \end{array}$$

4. 18 pizzas at 287¢ per pizza =

They would cost 5166¢,
which is \$51.66.

$$\begin{array}{r} 287 \\ \times\ 18 \\ \hline 2296 \\ \underline{287} \\ 5166 \end{array}$$

Chapter Nineteen
Sugar

We won't mention the honey cards.

Stanthony had planned on having all the 800 pizzas ready just after Fred finished his speech. There was, however, one pizza that was ready right now. It was Fred's 48-inch, no-topping, no-crust, no-cheese, no-sauce pizza.

Stanthony presented it to him.

Everyone else was jealous. They wanted to know why Fred got his pizza first. Then they realized that it was just an empty pizza pan.

No longer did they covet* Fred's being served first.

3:55 p.m.

Fred looked at the clock. It was five minutes to four. The conference was scheduled to start at four.

There was a last minute rush to buy things at the booths. At four, they would all close.

Some people were buying pencils, pens, paper, voice recorders, video cameras, and oil painting sets

---

* Covet = to go nuts over someone else's good fortune.

to capture the sounds and images of Math and Pizza Conference keynote presentation. This was a very special event. It only happened once every four years.

Even Prof. Eldwood was there. He had his trusty fountain pen and a bottle of blue-black ink so that he could take notes. About three months after each quadrennial conference, he would publish another volume in his series: *Math and Pizza Conference Notes.* Today's conference would become volume 40 in his series. Given his advanced age, Eldwood would often sit up close to the speaker so that he could hear more clearly.

Joe wandered over to the Sluice booth where a man was

shouting: "Step right up ladies and gentlemen. This is your chance of a lifetime. The Sluice Company is now offering its newest product: Sluice-in-the-Home. You never have to go to the store to buy Sluice, everyone's favorite soft drink.

"Each day, we will deliver a

Sluice-O-Matic

fresh five-gallon container for your Sluice-O-Matic machine to your house.

"Sluice is the world's most exciting lemon-lime soda. Don't confuse it with Slice® or Sprite® or Storm® or Seven-Up® or Sierra Mist® or Squirt®. Sluice is different. It has even more sugar than you could possibly imagine."

Joe interrupted him and asked, "How much sugar?"

The man with the megaphone smiled. "It depends on how much Sluice you want to make. If you don't want to make any, then you don't use any sugar. If you want to make a single serving, then you take 5 pounds of sugar and carefully add 7 drops of water to it."

"And how much sugar do you use to fill the five-gallon container?" Joe asked.

"We use 32 drops of water and. . . ."

At this point the house lights blinked off and on, off and on. It was the signal to close the booths. The conference was about to start.

Very briefly, Joe had been told (0 water, 0 sugar) and (7 drops of water, 5 pounds of sugar). If he graphed those two points, he'd have

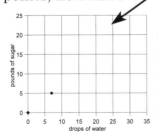

If he drew a line through those two points, he could guess that 32 drops would take about 23 pounds of sugar.

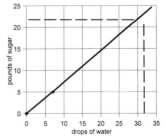

The television set that was mounted on the wall was turned off. People headed to their seats.

Some turned on their voice recorders. Some got out pencils and paper. Some started their video cameras. Prof. Eldwood unscrewed his fountain pen. One artist squeezed some dabs of oil paint onto his palette.

Elaine Marie had arrived from Polka Dot Publishing. She was there to introduce Fred as the keynote speaker for the conference.

When 800 people were wandering around before the conference started, she couldn't find three-foot-tall Fred. When everyone started to sit down, she spotted Fred. He had been watching a couple of minutes of the Marx Brothers' movie and was giggling.

He walked up to the speaker's platform and said, "Hello, Elaine Marie. I'm Fred."

"How did you know my name? Have we ever met?"

Fred pointed to the name tag she was wearing.

She asked, "I need to introduce you. What is the math or pizza topic that you've chosen?"

Fred straightened his pink bow tie and said, "Ice cream."

"But, but, but . . ." she sputtered.

[It looks like we have run out of room. This is where the index of the book is supposed to start. We'll continue, I promise, right here in the next book.]

Index

85-year calendar 13

ABCDEFG 70, 71, 73

area of a rectangle . . . 83, 84, 113

bar graphs 31

bibelots 25

big question in arithmetic . . . 15, 42, 72, 76, 120

borrowing one. 26

brass braces 113

capitalization in closing salutations 34

cardinality of a set 59

category theory, linear functionals, homeomorphisms 86

changing the scale on a graph 93

Chico Marx 86

codomain 95

collinear points 90

commutative law of union 101

converting ounces to pounds and ounces 115

converting seconds to minutes and seconds 119, 120

counting back the change 98-102, 113

counting possible combinations . . . 44, 47, 59, 64, 65, 116

covet—a definition.. 121

cryogenics 107

Cyprus on the map 56

division.. . . . . . . 67, 72, 90, 102

division by two-digit numbers 120

domain 95

drops, teaspoons, tablespoon, ounces, cups, quarts, gallons 70

elapsed time . . 39, 41, 45, 47, 64

empty set 60

estimating answers 116

examples of infinite sets 111

explicit statements 61

exponents 41, 42

expressing remainders as fractions 110

first coordinate 40, 74

flavors of ice cream 56

forest resources in the U.S. . . . 26

formal letters 33, 34

getting ice in the summer in
    Kansas in 1843 69

graph paper 108

graphing an ordered pair 74,
    75, 88, 93, 123

Greek alphabet 60

homogenized milk 106

Hooke's law 89

hyperbole 28

Iberian Peninsula 62

ibex 62

ice cream eating taught poorly
    84

imperial system 17

implicit statements 57

inequalities 103

Joe's stomach is not infinite
    111

KKKKK 58, 59

liberty is not the same as freedom
    101

literally true 52

m and cm don't require periods
    78

maps and artists 49

maps and cheese lovers 50

maps and historians of literature
    51

maps and mathematicians 50

maps and war historians 50

Marx Brothers' movie . . .86, 124

memory poem for 6 × 6 21

memory poem for 6 × 7 54

memory poem for 6 × 8 21

memory poem for 6 × 9 51

metric system 17, 66

Michelangelo 80

multiplying by a hundred . . . 114

multiplying by a two-digit
    number 16

numerals 42

ordered pairs 40, 74

parking on the sidewalk—why
    you shouldn't 76

peninsulas 62

perimeter when not all the
    dimensions are not on the
    map 82-84

personal letters 34, 35

Pizza Buttons 97-100

plotting points 93

poetry to help remember things
    14

polishing leather shoes 45

promised land vs. Wisconsin
    51

pronouncing French words that
    end in t 25

quadrennially 14

ream = 500 sheets 17, 28

reverie 55

samplers 75, 76

seat belts 73, 74

second coordinate 40, 74

seconds, minutes, hours in the
    metric system 66

sigma notation . . .
    . . . . 23, 24, 30, 47, 53

slope of a line 89

Sluice-in-the-Home 122, 123

special delivery emails 37

Index

Stanley Anthony—the story of
     his name 79, 80

subtracting centimeters from
     meters 77

subtracting feet from miles . . . 77

subtracting feet from yards . . 76,
            77

subtracting inches from feet and
     inches 53

subtracting minutes from hours
     48

subtracting ounces from gallons
     77

subtracting ounces from pounds
     . . . . 26, 35, 77

subtracting ounces from quarts
     110

superfluid is different than liquid
     107

troy ounces 17

why math was invented . . . 82, 83

why Stan couldn't fly 38

why the times sign is not used in
     algebra 44

why we use soap 106

x-coordinate 93

y-coordinate 93

If you would
like to read more
about Fred
or order books . . .

LifeofFred.com